the way

A PRACTICAL GUIDE
TO THE CHRISTIAN LIFE

**by Godfrey C. Robinson, B.A., B.D.
and Stephen F. Winward, M.A., B.D.**

SCRIPTURE UNION
130 City Road, London EC1V 2NJ

First published	–	*November* 1945
22nd Reprint	–	*November* 1977
Revised	–	*November* 1983

© *Stephen Winward and Mrs. G. Robinson*

ISBN 0 86201 142 6

Typesetting by Nuprint Services Ltd, Harpenden, Herts.
Printed in Great Britain by Ebenezer Baylis & Son Limited,
The Trinity Press, Worcester, and London.

Contents

Contents

Foreword

In their preface to the first edition the authors wrote:

'If any apology is needed for adding yet another to the already large number of books about the Christian life it will be found in the particular emphasis of this little volume.

In the general pastoral work of the church, and more especially in work among young people, the authors have long felt the need for a small handbook giving practical directions for Christian discipleship. There are, of course, many excellent treatises on the subject, but on examination they are frequently found to contain inspiring exhortations rather than practical instructions. And the young disciple is still left wondering how this attractive life can be lived. This book is neither an exhortation nor a description; it is intended as a guide-book, a Baedeker for the Christian Way.

It is our hope that the chapters will be of assistance in the instruction of candidates for Believers' Baptism, Confirmation and Church Membership. They should also be of value to any Christian who feels the need for directions regarding method and discipline. The book may be found suitable for group study and discussion, and questions (which can also be used for self-examination) have been supplied at the end of each chapter with this in view.'

This book is now reprinted in a revised form in the belief that it will help a new generation of Christians to grow towards maturity. Much is as fresh as when it was first written; where the original might have been a little obscure for the modern reader small changes have been made to make the meaning and impact clear. Biblical quotations, except where stated, are now from the New International Version.

1.
Introduction
The Christian Life

1

The purpose of this book about the Christian life can be expressed in one little word of three letters—*how!*

Imagine the case of a girl who once heard an inspiring broadcast talk on Beethoven's sonatas. In the course of the talk several excerpts were played by a famous pianist, and the girl was so thrilled with the music she heard that she immediately decided to learn to play the piano in order to have the joy of playing great music herself. As she possessed both a strong desire to play, and considerable, if latent, musical talent, it seemed that her efforts must be crowned with success. But now, years afterwards, the neighbours have to endure the daily agony of listening to Beethoven being murdered. What has happened to frustrate those noble intentions? In short, she never troubled to learn the technique, having resort neither to a teacher of music nor even a book of instruction. She never struggled with five-finger exercises, scales and such like, apart from which all the strong desire and latent talent in the world cannot produce fine music.

Many of us are not producing the music of fine Chrisian living for much the same reason. We also have heard inspiring descriptions of the Christian life, and have witnessed many attractive examples of it; we too have a strong desire to live for Christ, and have received the gift of the new life from his hands, and yet, in spite of all this, the result is often most disappointing, and the common reaction to our Christian living is not unlike that of the reaction of the neighbours in the illustration above.

The girl needed to learn *how* to play; the Christian needs to learn *how to live.* Attention must be given to method, to technique, to practice. Often we have listened to moving appeals to live the Christian life—rarely have we been told *how* to live it, *the end* has been painted for us in glowing colours, but *the means* to that end has been largely ignored. We are here concerned with the means, the method, the way to the end. It isn't possible, however, to describe *how* to live the Christian life without first asking, 'What is the Christian life?' We shall deal with this latter question first, and then return to consider *the means* in the clearer light afforded by the answer.

2

The word 'Christian' is used so vaguely and misused so widely nowadays, that it may be helpful to give a definition which is true to the teaching of our textbook, the New Testament. For, having defined this word, the meaning of the phrase 'the Christian life' will then be clear.

> A Christian is a person who has met God in Christ, and who is trusting in him as Saviour and obeying him as Lord.

The Christian life is thus a personal relationship. No one can grow or develop into this life; there must be encounter, crisis, decision, acceptance, committal. The analogy of marriage used in the New Testament is illuminating; two people *meet* and are attracted. The man woos the girl, she accepts (or, maybe, rejects) his proposal—in fact accepts him and gives herself to him, an acceptance which is sealed publicly in a covenant. Getting married is a definite act, and no man would dream of answering the question, 'Are you married?' by saying, 'I'm not quite sure, but I hope so!' Likewise a Christian is a person who has responded to

8

the initiative of the Saviour's redeeming love by a quite definite act of self-surrender, so entering into the 'new covenant'.

Now the relationship entered into by this act of self-committal has two aspects, described in the two sentences of our definition as 'trusting in him as Saviour', 'obeying him as Lord'. Many other phrases could be used to describe these two aspects, such as 'receiving and doing', 'resting and striving', but they all mean very much the same thing. There is that which God does, and there is that which we must do. For the Christian life is like the farmer's wheat harvest—it's entirely a gift of God, but taking possession of that gift requires hard work and strenuous effort. The girl of our first illustration had a musical gift, apart from which no amount of practice or technique would have made her musical; but her gift could only be made her own by practice. Both gift and practice are necessary. This is as true for the Christian as it is for the farmer or the musician. Let's consider the two aspects in turn.

'Trusting in him as Saviour.' The Christian life is a gift of God in Jesus Christ, and this gift must be *received* if it is to be possessed. We can never earn salvation by our own strenuous efforts, but we can receive it as a gift in humility, penitence and trust from God himself. This gift is Jesus Christ the Saviour, and 'he who has the Son has life'. He laid down his life at Calvary in order to redeem us from the penalty and power of sin.

> *'He died that we might be forgiven,*
> *He died to make us good,*
> *That we might go at last to heaven,*
> *Saved by his precious blood.'*

This life begins, then, when we receive Jesus Christ as Saviour; it continues as we live in him through faith. Through this union by faith with the Saviour, the Holy Spirit works out *in* us what Christ did *for* us on Calvary. By this working of the Holy Spirit alone are we brought out of death into life (regeneration), out of darkness into light (revelation), out of sin into holiness (sanctification). No dead man can make himself live, no blind man can make himself see. The Saviour through the operation of the Holy Spirit makes us what we are, and we depend absolutely, entirely, utterly upon him. The Christian life which begins with an *act* of receiving must continue as a life-long *attitude* of receiving. It is 'life in faith' and some of its great verbs are 'believing', 'receiving', 'abiding', 'trusting', 'depending', 'resting'.

'Obeying him as Lord'—that is the other side of the relationship. 'Unless the Lord builds the house, its builders labour in vain' (Psalm 127:1)—but 'they' must 'labour', for God does not build the house of our Christian character for us while we look idly on with folded hands. God does build—through our building; he does work in us when we stir ourselves to work out our own salvation. The work of the Holy Spirit within us depends for its continuance and perfection upon our response, our co-operation, our obedience. His creative action takes place through our obedient action, and he is able to work when we work. We are workers together with God. We have received the new life as a free gift, but we must practise the gift, if the music of fine Christian living is to result. It's therefore not possible to live a victorious life without obedient action, deliberate effort and careful discipline. As the New Testament also says, the Christian must 'fight', 'wrestle', 'run', 'work', 'suffer', 'endure', 'resist'— all words which clearly denote strenuous effort.

3

We have just described the Christian life as a personal relationship with the Lord Jesus Christ, having two main aspects—trusting and obeying, receiving and doing. But this knowledge does not of itself help us to live the life. For a vision of the *end,* however true and inspiring, is useless without a practical use of the *means* to that end. Sir Christopher Wren must have had a clear picture of St. Paul's Cathedral in his mind's eye before ever it was built, but the actual erection of the building involved the use of many practical and humble 'means'. We must go on then to consider the means by which Christian character is actually built to the glory of God, for his worship and service. That is to say, '*How* do we receive, *how* do we obey?'

Now we shall find in practice that these two aspects are so closely related that they cannot be separated. It's not therefore possible to isolate one group of activities in which we only receive, or another group in which we only obey. For example, prayer is undoubtedly a 'receiving', for by it we take the grace and power of God into our lives; but it's also a human 'doing', requiring method and discipline. So also witness is active human obedience to Christ, but it is also a means of receiving more fully the grace and truth of Christ. So with every aspect of the Christian life; we are all the time dealing with divine and human action. In this book we are therefore equally concerned with both aspects, and each chapter deals with one means, one method by which we both receive *and* obey.

What then are these 'means' or, to revert to an earlier illustration, what are the five-finger exercises and scales of the Christian life? We have attempted to describe the chief ones in the eight chapters of this book. They are the practice of prayer, the devotional reading of the Bible, personal discipline, overcoming temptation, seeking divine guidance, fellowship with other Christians, the service of others and witnessing for Christ. These *can* all be 'means of grace', overcoming temptation no less than Bible reading, service just as much as prayer, discipline as well as fellowship.

But to be such they must be practised. Merely to know about a thing isn't sufficient, and a Christian theorist will make little headway in spiritual living. 'Not everyone who says to me, "Lord, Lord," will enter the kingdom of heaven, but only he who *does* the will of my Father who is in heaven.' (Matt. 7:21). There must be immediate action; only 'practice makes perfect'. Paderewski, the world-famous Polish pianist, is reported to have said, 'If I stop practising the piano for a day, I notice the difference, if I stop for two days my family notices the difference, if I stop for three days my friends notice the difference, and if I stop for a week the public notices the difference.'

Here then is just a simple handbook containing eight lessons in Christian living, which *if practised* may help a little towards creating the thrilling music of fine and harmonious Christian living.

4

In the apostolic age Christianity was referred to as 'the way', which in accordance with Old Testament usage means conduct ordered by the laws of the Lord; a way of living involving the use of a definite discipline, the *method* of salvation. It would be a great gain if we could revert to this conception, for the alternative description, 'the faith', is apt to convey the impression that a Christian is one who holds all the correct views or doctrines. Now sound doctrine is, of course, of the utmost importance, for Christian living presupposes Christian conviction. The statement frequently made that 'it doesn't matter what a man believes so long as he acts rightly' is absurd, for belief is the ground and inspiration of conduct. Unfortunately, however, it is possible to have belief which does not express itself in conduct, in a way of life; this belief of the head, mere orthodoxy, is often confused with real faith. The latter, however, as we have seen, is a personal relationship of trust and obedience, and is therefore inseparable from conduct. A Christian really believes that which he acts upon, and it is in 'the way' that 'the faith' is best and most convincingly confessed.

This book is about the Christian way, and must therefore be mainly concerned with ordered conduct, practical disciplines, means and methods. But since these are only methods of trusting and obeying a Person, it is equally true to say that the whole book is about the Lord Jesus Christ our Saviour. For he is not only the end, he is also the way to the end; as the hymn puts it, 'Christ is the path, and Christ the prize'. And so we are concerned with Christ not only as the end to which all the method leads, but as *the method itself* at every stage. Since the Christian way is a personal way, its methods are personal. Like the movements of a great symphony, this book has a simple theme running throughout— *How* can I walk in him who said, 'I am the true and living way'?

2.

How to Pray

THIS CHAPTER TELLS YOU

We need to learn how to pray.

1. *The fixed times and places which are found to be most helpful.*

2. *The prayer-life may be stimulated and enriched by the use of certain helps. A list of these helps is given.*

3. *There are eight main types of prayer. How these may be combined in morning and evening prayers. How to plan a time with God.*

4. *How to pray with every aspect of our personality. The way to overcome feelings and moods.*

'One day Jesus was praying in a certain place. When he finished, one of his disciples said to him, "Lord, teach us to pray, just as John taught his disciples"' (Luke 11:1). In making this request, the disciples took it for granted that prayer is a necessity—having lived with the Lord Jesus they could not be ignorant of that fact—and asked rather to be taught how to pray. Now, we all need to be taught how to pray, but, unfortunately, unlike the disciples, we do not all realise this need.

It is surprising how many Christians quietly assume that there is nothing to be learnt about prayer and praying, and for this reason the prayer-life of many remains childish—which is by no means the same as childlike. We have to learn how to walk, ride a bicycle, play the piano, speak French and do many other things. Why then should we assume that the divine art of prayer does not need to be learnt? Jesus himself 'made his prayers and requests with loud cries and tears to God' (Hebrews 5:7, GNB) and left us not only an inspiring example, but also a rich deposit of teaching on the subject of prayer. Above all, he gave us the Holy Spirit to be our helper and teacher in this realm also: 'In the same way, the Spirit helps us in our weakness. We do not know what we ought to pray, but the Spirit himself intercedes for us with groans that words cannot express' (Rom. 8:26). Christ therefore teaches us how to pray, not only through his recorded words on that subject in the Gospels, but also through the Holy Spirit within us. All Christian prayer is prayer 'in the Spirit', since apart from him we cannot know the mind of God or co-operate with his purpose. He pleads with God on behalf of his people and in accordance with his will (Rom. 8:27, GNB), and this intercession is made through the hearts and lips of those who 'pray on every occasion, as the Spirit leads' (Eph. 6:18, GNB).

But, of course, the Holy Spirit is not just a personal possession; he indwells the whole fellowship of Christ, and for that reason his teaching often comes to us through that fellowship. Many following in the steps of Jesus have walked this path before us, and have left to us, 'the heirs of all the ages', a rich deposit of wisdom and experience. Into this great devotional heritage we must seek to enter, believing that the divine teacher, who spoke to them through the Spirit and was to them an ever-present help and guide, will also 'teach us to pray'.

1—Time and place

In the worship of the Old Covenant, the daily sacrifice was offered early in the morning and again at evening. Peter appeals to the people of the New Covenant to 'come as living stones, and let yourselves be used in building the spiritual temple, where you will serve as holy priests to offer spiritual and acceptable sacrifices to God through Jesus Christ' (I Pet. 2:5, GNB). Christians are priests, privileged to offer to God through Christ the spiritual sacrifices of praise and prayer—every day, in the morning and in the evening. This is our 'continual offering'.

'Every day, in the morning and in the evening'—but if this is to be done we must set aside time for morning and evening prayer, and be very definite and practical. Nothing that is said about prayer will be of much use unless definite times are set aside for it. If this isn't done, it will simply be crowded out of our lives by the demands of the busy and hectic modern world. Prayer is often neglected, not because Christians disbelieve in it, but because they have never *set aside* definite times for it. Now, the natural times for daily prayer, although of course not the only times, are early in the morning after rising from sleep, and again in the evening, at the close of the day's work.

If adequate time is to be given to prayer each morning before the day's work begins, we must discipline ourselves to get up at the required hour. An alarm-clock is the first piece of equipment needed in the prayer-life! Unless we learn to get up from bed at the fixed hour, a disciplined prayer-life is just not possible.

Before breakfast will be the ideal time for most people; sometimes, owing to domestic arrangements, it may be necessary to have prayer-time after breakfast, especially if it takes the form of family prayers. The problem of time is not usually so urgent in the evening; isn't it a pity, however, to offer God the 'fag end' of the day, when one is probably feeling very tired, and the desire for sleep may be stronger than the desire to pray? Why not try having evening prayers immediately after the main evening meal, which most families have on coming home from work? At such a time the mind is still fresh, and concentration is easier.

What length of time should be set aside for prayer in the morning and in the evening? This is a difficult question to answer, because the answer is not the same for everyone. Half-an-hour is certainly not too long; anything less than ten minutes is certainly too short. It is wise at first not to set an impossibly high ideal; aim at fifteen to twenty minutes, and then try later to extend it to half-an-hour or more. It is wise not to cram too much into the available time, for it is impossible to pray in a hurry; rather, we must learn 'to wait patiently for God'. When the morning and evening periods have been fixed, keeping faithfully to them should be regarded as part of one's loyalty to Christ, for prayer is not a daily duty, but a personal meeting with the one we love.

As to the *place* of prayer—this will often depend on family arrangements and the size of the house. Ideally, a quiet room other than one's bedroom is best; but if no such room is available, the bedroom must be used. It is helpful, if possible, to have a prayer corner, consisting perhaps of a small table, against which one can kneel, for the Bible and other devotional books. Such a corner soon comes to have helpful suggestions. During the warmer months we may follow our Lord's example and seek some quiet spot out of doors for prayer and meditation; or some church near our home or place of work. The essential thing to aim at in this connection is quiet and freedom from interruption: 'When you pray, go into your room, close the door and pray to your Father, who is unseen' (Matt. 6:6).

2—The use of helps

Many Christians find it difficult to know what to say in their prayers, and often find themselves repeating the same phrases and ideas. It is easy to get into the habit of using pious 'catch' phrases which may have very little meaning, and of saying to God the same sort of thing each day until it becomes thoroughly unreal. The main solution to this difficulty is to live in such intimate fellowship with God through Jesus Christ that we cannot but be real and sincere in his presence. And if we bring to God in prayer the various aspects of daily life, with its interests and variety, prayer is unlikely to become stale or unreal.

In addition to these suggestions, monotony and narrowness of interest in the prayer-life may be avoided by making full use of the rich and varied devotional heritage which has come down to us.

Before going on to suggest how this may be done, it is necessary to stress that the prayers of others should never be used as a *substitute* for our own personal prayers. They may be used to *supplement* them, and if this is done they can be of great value in teaching us to make our own prayers more perfect. Nothing can ever take the place of personal prayer, and the written prayers of others should help us to create our own. But this does not mean that we cannot *pray* the prayers of others; Christians have always done so, the 'Lord's Prayer' itself being the supreme example.

Here, in fact, two extremes are to be avoided; to depend entirely on the written prayers of others on the one hand, to rely entirely on our own prayers on the other. In the former case there is real danger of becoming mechanical and quenching the freedom and spontaneity of the Spirit; in the latter, the prayer-life is apt to become narrow and monotonous, and at the mercy of passing moods. The ideal is to use forms of prayer as a framework for one's own prayers.

The available material to help us in prayer may be classified under four heads.

(a) *The Bible.* All prayer-life should be based upon and related to the Bible, for we are to speak to God upon the basis of what he says to us in his word. In this way prayer becomes a dialogue instead of a monologue. We shall attempt to show in the next chapter on Bible study just how Bible reading and prayer are related, so there is no need to enter into further detail here. The point is of vital importance, for prayer without the Bible is bound to become thin, unreal and in the end unchristian.

(b) *The book of Psalms* has been the praise and prayer book of temple, synagogue and church in all ages, and every Christian should learn how to use it in daily prayer. We do not mean merely that a psalm should be read; it should be prayed on our knees. It should be repeated aloud as an offering of praise and prayer to God. The reader is advised to make his own collection of psalms which can thus be used in personal prayer, marking them in his Bible, for not all the psalms are equally suitable for use in this particular way.

(c) *Hymn books* are fine collections of prayers of all kinds, and are especially helpful for praise and thanksgiving. It is a good thing to sing a selected hymn to God, but, if the reader is afraid of the sound of his own voice, the hymn may be said as a prayer, kneeling. Every Christian should possess and use his own church hymn book and perhaps a book of contemporary songs of praise.

(d) *Books of prayers*. There are available now many helpful collections of prayers. We commend to you those books published by your own church or tradition.

3—The chief kinds of prayer

When a ray of sunlight is passed through a triangular glass prism, it is broken up into all the colours of the spectrum from red to violet. The white heavenly light of prayer can also be broken up by the human mind into eight main parts. Each of these parts should be included in any complete prayer-life.

(1) *Praise* or *adoration* is the expression of pure love to God, and is the highest form of prayer. It is to delight in his being and attributes, 'to glorify God and enjoy him', to acknowledge his supreme *worth* (see Ps. 145). In offering this, the psalms and the hymn book are our two chief helps.

(2) *Thanksgiving* is the grateful acknowledgment of our indebtedness to him who gives 'every good and perfect gift'; it is saying 'thank you' to God. The Christian should make a daily practice of this, and not take God's gifts for granted.

(3) *Penitence*. Man always approaches God as a sinner in need of forgiveness, through the redeeming work of Jesus Christ. True penitence includes *self-examination*, or the searching of the heart before God; *confession*, which is making known in words our sin to God, and this should be made not in vague general terms, but in full detail; the request for *pardon*, which should be consciously received while still kneeling, trusting in what the Saviour has done (see Psalm 51).

(4) *Intercession* is praying for other people, and here the believer joins in the prayers of his exalted High Priest, who lives for ever to make intercession for us. In fellowship with the Lord we, 'a royal priesthood', pray for our fellow Christians and for the whole

world. It is most helpful to keep a list of the people for whom one ought especially to pray, and to mark opposite each name the date on which prayer was last made for that one.

(5) *Petition* is making our own personal requests to God the Father, who desires to know and to satisfy the needs of all his children. Such requests must be according to the will or purpose of God, and, when this condition is fulfilled, we must pray believing that God will grant them.

(6) *Consecration* is the offering or dedication of the whole self as a 'living sacrifice' to God (Rom. 12:1) and is the climax of all prayer. Each morning the believer should make such a full surrender, dedicating himself to God for the coming day.

In these six forms of prayer the believer addresses God. But Christian prayer is not a one-way conversation; God also speaks to us, if we allow him, in a properly directed prayer-time. And so to these six types of prayer we must add two more.

(7) *Meditation on Scripture,* through which God speaks to us by the Holy Spirit, implanting convictions in the mind and heart. We shall consider this more fully in the next chapter on Bible reading.

(8) *Guidance.* We use this word to describe the directions God gives to us when a quiet review of the coming day, or of any problem or situation, is made in his presence. In this way especially our prayers are related to our daily life, and issue in that obedient action which should be the consequence of all true prayer.

Now, these eight types should all find a place in our daily prayers, and they can be arranged and combined in various ways. The reader may make his own daily orders of prayer, and vary them from time to time. It is sometimes valuable to spend a whole prayer-time on one of these aspects, *e.g.* Saturday evening prayer might consist entirely of 'penitence'—a full self-examination, followed by confession. We outline one such daily order as a pattern of what is meant:

1. Praise or adoration (from the Psalms or hymn book, or in one's own words).
2. Bible reading, and meditation.
3. Petition (for the coming day).
4. Dedication of oneself to God.

1. Bible reading.
2. Quiet review of the day—this will provide material for:
3. Penitence (confession of any sin or negligence today),
4. Intercession (for those you have met or those in need),
5. Thanksgiving (for God's goodness today).

The advantage of such order in prayer is evident; prayer ceases to be a jumble of words, a jungle of unrelated sentences. Rather, the mind has a clear understanding of just what is being done at each stage. After all, there is something to be said for the little boy who finished his evening prayers with the words: 'That is all for tonight, and here are the headlines again'!

4—Total prayer

The first and great commandment of the prayer-life, as of all life, is 'Love the Lord your God with all your heart and with all your soul and with all your mind and with all your strength' (Mark 12:30). Man must worship and serve God with the *whole* of his personality, and not merely with some part of it.

In this connection the most common mistake is to imagine that prayer is entirely a matter of the feelings or emotions. This is the error of the person who says, 'I only pray when I feel like it', the assumption being that prayer is real only in such circumstances. This is a disastrous mistake, for the feelings of any person are by nature changing and inconstant; they rise and fall like the temperature chart of a fever-stricken patient. For this reason any attempt to build a prayer-life *on them alone* is like building a house on the shifting sands.

Of course, feeling is one essential element in a complete prayer-life, and we *are* to love God emotionally—but the part is not the whole, and we must never rely upon what is the most unreliable aspect of our human nature. If a Christian does so, he will most certainly fall into 'the slough of despond', and become the victim of his own changing moods. Now, moods are public enemy number one in the prayer-life, and one of our first tasks is to learn how to overcome them. They are sure to come—even the greatest saints knew them—but they can be conquered by accepting the discipline of a rule such as the following: 'I intend to pray to God every day at the fixed times, *whatever I feel like.*' With my feelings, without my feelings, or if necessary against my feelings —I will worship God.

To say this is to affirm the fact that the *will* is the primary thing in the life of prayer—although it is not the only thing. That is the meaning of the phrase 'with all your heart', for to the Hebrews 'the heart' meant not primarily the emotions, but the will. Now, there can be no regular and ordered prayer-life apart from the will, the fixed, resolute determination to have it. The worship of God begins with the will to worship him, and this must express itself in a regular, ordered, systematic devotional life—in fact, in a rule of prayer. The will is the rock upon which the house of the prayer-life is built.

But here again, 'the will' is not the only aspect of prayer, and without the 'mind' or intelligence it can easily degenerate into mere formalism. We are to offer to God a 'reasonable' sacrifice, using thought and imagination to the utmost in our prayers. Not even the body should be excluded from prayer, since our outward attitudes and actions have a deep influence on the inner life. To 'kneel before the Lord our Maker', to 'worship and fall down', to 'lift up holy hands' in prayer, to cover the face with the hands, like the seraphim of Isaiah's vision, before the divine glory; to sing out our praises, to say aloud our prayers—these are some of the ways in which the body can help us to pray. For man is not pure spirit, but a body also, and must learn to worship his Creator and Redeemer with every part and aspect of his created and redeemed nature.

Such 'total prayer' (like 'total war') can never be an easy task; but let us never forget that we always have two divine helpers. For in all Christian prayer we draw near by faith to the holy place where our Saviour makes perpetual intercession for us, and at the same time the Holy Spirit prays within us and through us. In the power of the Spirit, the advocate within, we unite our prayers with the powerful, all-availing intercession of our advocate with the Father, and make that total self-offering which is the climax and the fulfilment of all prayer—'offer your bodies as living sacrifices, holy and pleasing to God—which is your spiritual worship' (Rom. 12:1).

Questions

1. *'I only pray when I am in the mood for it.' How do you react to this statement?*
2. *Think about the use and misuse of written prayers.*
3. *How should prayer be related to Bible reading?*
4. *How would you reconcile practical instruction on prayer (this chapter, for example) with the promise that the Holy Spirit will teach us all things?*
5. *How would you tackle (a) dryness, (b) wandering thoughts, (c) self-centredness, (d) monotonous repetition, in the prayer-life?*
6. *Suggest a number of different outlines for morning and evening prayer.*
7. *In what different ways is prayer related to daily life?*

3.

How to Read the Bible

THIS CHAPTER TELLS YOU

1. *The reason why we should read the Bible.*

2. *The right frame of mind in which to read the Bible. The necessity for using all our faculties in order to get the best out of a selected passage.*

3. *There are a number of helps to aid us in our understanding of the Bible. A list of these helps is given.*

4. *An outline plan for making a start.*

5. *How to proceed further with Bible study; practical suggestions as to study courses. The necessity for perseverance.*

1—Why read the Bible

The purpose of the Bible is to testify to the Lord Jesus Christ. Just as John the Baptist pointed to Christ with the words, 'Look, the Lamb of God, who takes away the sin of the world!' (John 1:29), so the Bible exists to point men to him, the only Saviour.

The Bible, therefore, is not an end in itself, but a means whereby we come to Christ, the living Word of God; and the chief purpose of the book is to bring us to the Person. The words which describe the purpose of the Gospel of John may rightly be used of the whole Bible: 'These are written, that you may believe that Jesus is the Christ, the Son of God, and that by believing you may have life in his name' (John 20:31).

We study the Bible, then, in order that we may come into personal contact with the Lord Jesus Christ and, putting our whole trust in him, live obediently to his word. This is just what Jesus himself taught us about the purpose of scripture: 'You diligently study the Scriptures because you think that by them you possess eternal life. These are the Scriptures that testify about me, yet you refuse to come to me to have life' (John 5:39, 40). In these words we learn with deep simplicity the purpose of all Bible study—'study the Scriptures . . . come to me to have life.'

It is necessary to stress this truth, that the purpose of Bible reading is personal encounter, personal meeting with Jesus Christ. The Bible may of course be studied in other ways, but it does not speak to our hearts then as the living word of God. If we study 'the Bible designed to be read as literature', or as a book of ancient history or biography, then the 'veil remains' (2 Cor. 3:14). Nor do we read the Bible to find out a lot *about* God, but rather to find God himself revealed in Jesus Christ.

Now, it is of course possible and indeed easy to read the Bible without coming into personal contact with the living God revealed in Jesus Christ, and to fall under his condemnation, 'You . . . study the Scriptures . . . yet you *refuse* to come to *me*.' There is little virtue or value in merely reading something from the Bible every day; that in itself will not help us become vital Christians. It depends on *why* we read it, and *how* we read it. As Luther says, 'Christ is the Lord and King of scripture', and as we go to the cradle only for the sake of the baby (Luther's own metaphor), so also we go to scripture—for Christ. The purpose of daily Bible reading, therefore, is to meet God in Christ, and to be addressed by him through the Holy Spirit.

2—How to read

Now, if this purpose is to be realised, the Bible must be read in a certain way. First of all, there must be *reverence* in our approach, for if the Bible is to be an interview with the living God it cannot be read with one's feet on the mantlepiece or slouching in an easy chair. It may be helpful sometimes to read it kneeling.

Secondly, we should come to it with a high level of *expectancy,* believing that we *shall* meet with 'the God and Father of our Lord Jesus Christ', and that he will speak to us through the words of scripture. So often God is prevented from revealing himself, simply because we do not look for him to do so.

Thirdly, there must be *dependence* on the work of the Holy Spirit, for he alone can interpret scripture and reveal Christ to us. The veil hangs over all scripture until we turn to 'the Lord . . . the Spirit', and then 'the veil is taken away' (2 Cor. 3:16, 17). It is wise, therefore, to begin with a prayer for the Spirit's help—'Come, Holy Ghost . . . unlock the truth, Thyself the key; unseal the sacred book.'

If we do thus come with reverence towards God, expecting to meet the Lord Christ, the living Word, and depending on the Holy Spirit to reveal him, then the scripture we read will 'find' us and 'speak' to our condition. Every Bible lover will understand the meaning of these two words, although it is far from easy to explain their meaning. Our reading, or some part of the passage, will stand out for us, and apply itself to our condition. The book comes to life, and speaks; or, to put it more accurately, Christ the living Word actually speaks through the words. By the phrase 'actually speaks', it is of course not implied that we hear audible words. God speaks by implanting convictions; they may be convictions of truth, convictions of sin, or convictions of positive duty. Such convictions are the language of the Spirit of God.

To read the Bible in this way requires adequate *time.* It must be read in leisurely fashion, and not with one's eye on the clock; we must learn to '*wait* on the Lord', and to attend to him quietly and patiently if we are to be addressed by him through the book. Adequate time must therefore be set aside either during morning prayers or some time in the evening. It is better to read unhurriedly in the evening than to rush through a passage in the morning. The value of reading the Bible in a hurry is practically nil!

The week should be so planned that there are definite set periods, short or long as circumstances permit, when this unhurried reading can be enjoyed. However, even with adequate time, it is still possible to read the Bible too quickly, to skim over the surface instead of mining for the gold hidden in its depths. The following further suggestions will be found helpful:

(a) Read only a short passage at a time. Many people make the mistake of reading too much at one sitting; there is little value in merely reading through the Bible or a book of the Bible in minimum time; it is better to have a thorough appreciation of one picture in the art gallery than to 'do' the whole gallery—and see none of them. A chapter is always sufficient and is usually too much for one sitting. Take just one incident or one paragraph, and let that suffice.

(b) Read through the passage slowly, using the *intellect* fully in order to grasp its meaning, and asking all kinds of questions about it. Make sure that you understand it, and, if you do not, determine to find out by asking someone else, or by using a commentary. It may be helpful to compare similar passages which come to mind, or are suggested by the references in your Bible.

(c) If the reading is a story or incident, proceed to make a vivid picture of the scene in the mind by using the *imagination*. Look in turn at all the characters and *see* the action of the story. It is very important in living the Christian life that the word of God should capture our imagination. Having made the picture, look at it as long as possible, so that the scene may sink deeply into the mind.

(d) Ask what God is saying to you through the passage, and how it applies to your own life and present situation. Note especially any sentences which 'find' you, 'strike' you, or 'speak' to you, and ask what practical directions God is giving to you for your present life. Make a practice of obeying and carrying out these directions, because the reason for hearing the word of God is that we may do it (Matt. 7:24). Many have found it helpful to have a notebook in which to write down each day these convictions

26

and directions; in this way a permanent record is made of truth one has seen, and it also serves as a reminder of the directions God has given for obedient action.

3—The use of helps

The only help needed in reading the Bible is that of the Holy Spirit, the revealer and interpreter; he who gave the word alone can rightly interpret it. But the Holy Spirit often works through a human agent, as when he interpreted the scriptures to the Ethiopian through Philip (Acts 8:34, 35). We must not therefore despise the helps which the Spirit provides, but rather receive them gratefully as gifts from him.

There are many parts of the Bible that can be understood without any outside help, because the meaning, although profound, is obvious. No one, for example, finds any difficulty in understanding the history of the books of Samuel, or the stories of the Gospels. It is, of course, true that even in such instances other people can help us to a fuller and deeper understanding, and we should never hesitate to avail ourselves of such help.

On the other hand, there are many parts of the Bible for the right understanding of which outside help is a necessity. It is, for example, unlikely that the beginner will be able to make very much of the prophecies of Nahum or Zechariah, or the Books of Daniel or Revelation without a knowledge of the historical background. The Bible is an Eastern book written by Easterners with their particular background. This means that any helps which shed light on the Eastern pictures will assist us in understanding what the Bible has to teach.

It may at first appear strange that this book, which is able to make us 'wise for salvation' (2 Tim. 3:15), should thus contain 'some things that are hard to understand' (2 Pet. 3:16), but it must be remembered that the Bible is the book of the people of God, the church of Christ. The God who gave us the book has also given us the fellowship to help in interpreting the book; the Holy Spirit who inspired it dwells in the fellowship which reads it. In this fellowship the Holy Spirit himself has ordained and appointed certain members of the Body to preach, teach, and interpret; and the inspired book and the Spirit-indwelt fellowship with its inspired teachers belong together—and 'what God has joined together let no man separate.' 'Do you understand what you are reading?' . . . 'How can I . . . unless someone explains it to me?' (Acts 8:30, 31.) To anyone in such difficulty over any part of scripture, God has appointed human teachers and interpreters to 'come up and sit with him.'

Now in practice this means two things. First we must study the Bible not only privately, but also with and in the Christian fellowship. If we make a point of meeting with other Christians for regular Bible study and teaching we will be helped towards a right understanding of the Bible. In addition to the regular Sunday worship service try to get to the meeting during the week which is held specifically for the purpose of the Bible study. If no such meeting exists in your locality, it is always possible to form a group for Bible study—perhaps meeting in your own home. Great help and inspiration can be derived from learning together in this way.

Second, the Bible may be studied with the help of commentaries and other books, written in order to interpret its meaning. Many such excellent works on all parts of the Bible exist nowadays; indeed the number is so large that one cannot begin to give examples without adding another book to this already large number. As an ancient Jewish writer once said, 'of making many books there is no end!'

Here it is perhaps necessary to utter a word of warning; it is very easy to fall into the habit of reading books about the Bible instead of reading the Bible. But Bible study is the study of the Bible, not of books about the Bible. It is also necessary to add that, while there are many books which help to interpret the Bible, there are unfortunately just as many that misinterpret it. John's advice, 'do not believe every spirit, but test the spirits to see whether they are from God' (1 John 4:1), applies likewise to books; we must judge the book by the Bible, and not the Bible by the book. In the selection of such books it is advisable to ask the advice of one's minister, or of some other wise and trusted Christian friend.

There are many versions of the Bible in English today—perhaps too many! We recommend the Revised Standard Version, the New English Bible, the Good News Bible, and the New International Version. In these, the results of contemporary scholarship are expressed in good, intelligible English. It is also helpful to have one or two free translations or paraphrases. These not only help us to understand the more difficult books of the Bible, they can also bring a familiar—perhaps too familiar in the bad sense—passage home with a fresh impact, giving new insight into its meaning. They can be especially helpful to the beginner, but should not be used as a permanent substitute for the standard versions. As free translations or paraphrases of the original Hebrew or Greek, they have originality, relevance and freshness. The standard versions have greater literary worth, dignity and accuracy. It is wise to use both.

It is most helpful to make written notes on the various books of the Bible, whether of one's own meditations or of knowledge obtained from talks, study groups or commentaries. If possible, have a Bible with wide margins, so that the main outline or divisions of the book may be written in, together with any notes of interpretation. For more extensive notes a notebook will be necessary, but there is a great advantage in having the notes in the Bible itself, so that they are *there* when the book is being read. After all, your Bible is *your* Bible!

4—Making a start

When reading an ordinary book, we start at the beginning and read through continuously to the end, and this would seem to be the obvious way to read the Bible. Many start out enthusiastically in this way, but not so many get past the complex passages in Leviticus or the first ten chapters of Chronicles.

There is a wiser and better method. As was said at the beginning, we read the Bible to come to Christ the living Word. He is present in all scripture, but it is better to begin where we see him most clearly—that is, in the New Testament, particularly in the Gospels. He who lies hidden in the Old Testament is revealed in the New; when we have seen him in the latter, we shall find him in the former. For example, the Book of Leviticus does testify to the person and work of Jesus Christ, as we see in the interpretation of it given in the epistle to the Hebrews; so by reading from the latter first, we are much more likely to understand the former. It is true, we cannot *fully* understand either book apart from the other (and this is so of the Old and New Testaments as a whole), but it is better to begin with the New Testament, and to read the Old Testament afterwards in the light of its fulfilment.

It is better to begin with the New Testament—and it is best to begin with the Gospels. From the latter may be obtained a knowledge of the life, teaching, death, and resurrection of Christ, and this is the foundation of all Christian and biblical knowledge. Begin by reading the Gospel of Mark, which is the earliest and shortest account of the ministry and passion of Jesus. This may be followed by the Gospels of Matthew and Luke, which supplement and expand the story as told by Mark. The Gospel of Luke should be followed by the Acts of the Apostles, which is Volume 2 of the same work, and is a history of the early church. It is wise not to tackle any other part of the New Testament before studying the first three gospels and the Acts; it is also worth while taking time to acquire a good knowledge of their contents before proceeding to more advanced courses of study.

When these first steps have been taken, there are many ways in which Bible study may be continued.

5—Study courses

If we are to avoid reading at random and going over our own favourite passage repeatedly it is important that we follow a system. For the devotional reading of the Bible, daily readings and helpful notes may be obtained from the Scripture Union. In this system the readings are normally selected consecutively from one book. There is great advantage in reading through one book in order, and in having some outside help in its interpretation and application to our lives.

Other systems of daily readings are available. Many churches have someone who is responsible for obtaining and distributing Scripture Union notes or other schemes. Most are available from Christian bookshops. If you are in doubt your minister or an experienced Christian friend will be able to advise you.

Another excellent method is to select one of the great biblical themes such as Salvation, the Holy Spirit, the Messsiah, the Covenant, etc., and with the help of a concordance look up all references and study the relevant passages. In this connection a book of systematic theology will prove a helpful guide, in addition to suggesting such themes.

It will be found that most of the books of the Bible fall into groups having the same human author, or the same historical background, or the same essential characteristics. It will therefore be helpful not merely to study individual books, but whole groups at a time. Here are some examples of what is meant—the three synoptic Gospels, Mark, Matthew, Luke; the Gospel and letters of John; the letters of Paul in chronological order; apocalyptic literature, e.g. Daniel, Revelation; the Hebrew prophets in correct time order; the Wisdom literature, e.g. Proverbs, Ecclesiastes, Job; the books of the Law; the historical books; books which belong together, e.g. Leviticus and Hebrews. Find out the natural groupings and plan your reading and study accordingly.

Whether the reader adopts one of these systems or makes his own, it *is* necessary to have a system for Bible study. The habit of turning the pages and reading anywhere without plan, like a seagull dipping here and there into the sea of truth, cannot be compared with the value of ordered, planned reading. Without such a plan, the reader is liable to confine his reading to the 'purple passages' of the Bible, and to ignore all the other parts. But the Bible does not consist of a number of isolated 'texts' or disconnected passages; it is the written record of the revealing and redeeming activity of God in the history of Israel, and in the coming of Jesus Christ. It must therefore be studied as a whole.

It is true that the reader will not find every part of the Bible equally interesting, and it may be that *at first* some parts will appear to be dull and monotonous. No part of the Bible *is* in fact dull, but because of our blindness it may often seem so to us—at first. We must never make the mistake of concluding that because we see little or nothing in a particular part of the Bible, therefore there *is* nothing actually there. Let us rather dig more deeply for the hidden gold, until the biblical description of the miner becomes true of us—'his eyes see all its treasures' (Job 28:10).

It is for this reason that Bible reading presupposes that quality so necessary in every part of the Christian life—perseverance, the ability to go on and on. It is very easy to make a start like Christian in *The Pilgrim's Progress,* who began his journey when he 'opened the book and read therein'; but we must learn, like Christian, to go on up the Hill Difficulty, on over desolate moors, to rejoice on the mountain-tops, to go on through dark valleys— but at all costs to keep on, 'looking unto Jesus', the living and abiding Word of God, to whom, as 'Author and Finisher', the whole book points us.

Questions

1. *Why should we read the Bible?*
2. *What is meant by saying that 'God speaks to us in the Bible'?*
3. *Why do so many Christians neglect Bible reading?*
4. *Is there any value in reading the Bible just as literature, history, poetry, biography, etc.?*
5. *What directions would you give to a young convert starting to read the Bible?*
6. *'The Holy Spirit is the interpreter of scripture; therefore human help is unnecessary.' Think about this statement.*
7. *'Reading the Bible bores me.' What reply would you make to this statement?*

4.

How to Lead a Disciplined Life

THIS CHAPTER TELLS YOU

1. *What God does and what you have to do in the Christian life.*

2. *The thought-life is the well-spring of action. Discipline therefore must begin with the mind. The relation between discipline and discipleship.*

3. *The unruly member, the tongue, can become a servant instead of a master by the application of a few simple rules.*

4. *How to make the best use of your time. The use of a diary and the need for planning.*

5. *The Christian is the steward, and not the owner, of his possessions. The right way of budgeting and spending money.*

6. *How to control the bodily appetites. The place of physical exercise and recreation.*

1—Receiving and doing

The reader will remember that in the introductory chapter

attention was drawn to the fact that the Christian life has two main aspects. These we described as 'receiving' and 'doing'. It is fatal to ignore either of these aspects, or to emphasise one at the expense of the other. On the one hand, God through Jesus Christ has done something for us; we become Christians only by *receiving* that which he has done, and by 'resting in the finished work of Christ'.

On the other hand, these gifts of God can be received and appropriated only by human effort and discipline. Salvation is a free gift—but we must 'work out...our salvation'; the Holy Spirit is a free gift—but we must 'walk in the Spirit'. We must therefore beware of the mistake so often made of setting up these complementary aspects of the Christian life as contradictories. We must rest, remain, trust, receive—we must also make every effort, fight, run, take hold and work; these are all New Testament verbs.

Now, in this chapter we are concerned with the second aspect of the Christian life—that which the Christian himself must do. He must do something—but he cannot do it by himself. All that we here write presupposes the redeeming work of Christ and the present activity of the Holy Spirit. 'What the Gospel does is to set human action in its right relation to the action of God; right human action is always in the nature of a response to the prior action of God.' As Paul perfectly expressed it, 'I can do everything through him who gives me strength' (Phil. 4:13).

'I can do'—and I must do! The Christian must take himself in hand, he must shoulder responsibility for himself, he must set out to make something of life; he must prepare his mind 'for action' (1 Peter 1:13) and work out his own salvation. In a word, he must tackle himself and the business of Christian living—and that means personal discipline. Without such a serious intention and effort, no progress can be made in Christian discipleship. The Master himself said: 'small is the gate and narrow the road that leads to life, and only a few find it' (Matt. 7:14); it is the way of discipline, renunciation and hardship. The Christian is a soldier who must 'endure hardship' (2 Tim. 2:3), a boxer who 'practises self-restraint all round...and mauls and masters' his own body

34

(1 Cor. 9:25, 27 Moffatt), an athlete who must 'strip off every handicap' and run with patient endurance (Heb. 12:1, Moffatt). It is our purpose now to indicate in greater detail just what this involves for a disciple of Christ today. We should, however, always remember that discipline in the Christian life is not an end in itself, it is a means to the greater objective of being transformed into the image of God's Son. We discipline ourselves that we might develop a closer relationship with Christ and experience the life of his Spirit in greater measure. No matter how disciplined our lives, if we are not, above all else, longing to be filled with the Spirit of Christ and the love of Christ we shall not benefit at all.

2—The mind

'Prepare your mind for action'—in this delightful, mixed, but expressive metaphor the apostle Peter indicates to us where all real discipline must begin. He is but echoing the words of his Saviour: 'Be dressed ready for service and keep your lamps burning' (Luke 12:35). There is to be about the Christian a certain mental alertness, a quickness of perception. The disciple must be mentally and spiritually awake: 'Let us not be like others, who are asleep, but let us be alert and self-controlled' (1 Thess. 5:6).

The training and discipline of the mind is an essential part of Christian discipleship. The original meaning of the word translated 'disciple' was 'learner', 'pupil', 'scholar', 'student', and Christ invited men to himself in these terms: 'Come to me... and learn from me' (Matt. 11:28, 29). The connection between the words 'disciple' and 'discipline' is evident; it is significant that the subjects of a school curriculum used to be called 'the disciplines'. We are to come to Christ and learn of him, taking upon ourselves the discipline of his 'yoke', and the result will be a mind informed with divine wisdom, sensitive to all truth, watchful against all evil.

The discipline of the outer life depends entirely upon this discipline of the inner life—that is, the discipline of the mind. A man's actions whether good or evil are but the outcome of his inner life of thought and desire. It is not possible in the long run to fill the mind with evil, and then do good, for 'a good tree cannot bear bad fruit, and a bad tree cannot bear good fruit' (Matt. 7:18). 'For from within, out of men's hearts, come evil thoughts'—and bear as fruit those terrible actions which the Lord then lists (Mark 7:21, 22); 'all these evils come from inside.'

Now the Christian, who has been given a new heart and a new nature, must take and possess the gift by turning his mind and directing his attention to the things of Christ, and away from the things of evil. 'Those who live according to the sinful nature have their minds set on what that nature desires; but those who live in accordance with the Spirit have their minds set on what the Spirit desires' (Rom. 8:5). By the discipline of the mind, we mean this redirection of the attention. Negatively, the mind must be turned away from all evil; positively, there must be an active setting of our minds 'on things above'. This is done by means of a regular devotional life, reading the Bible and other good and uplifting books, the practice of recollection or recalling the presence of Christ during the day, fellowship with other Christians, and Christian work and service.

These are some of the channels through which the power of Christ reaches us. Just as there are definite roads and railways as the shortest ways of reaching certain destinations, so we must understand that there are distinctive 'means of grace' through which the spiritual life is nourished. It is useless to profess to be following Christ, or to complain that spiritual life is a failure, if all the time the means of grace are being neglected. 'Whatever is true... noble... right... pure... lovely... admirable—if any-thing is excellent or praiseworthy—think about such things' (Phil. 4:8). That which holds your attention, holds you; 'we, who... contemplate the Lord's glory, are being transformed into his likeness' (2 Cor. 3:18, NIV margin).

3—The unruly member

'... Take ships as an example. Although they are so large and are driven by strong winds, they are steered by a very small rudder wherever the pilot wants to go. Likewise the tongue is a small part of the body, but it makes great boasts. Consider what a great forest is set on fire by a small spark. The tongue also is a fire . . . a restless evil, full of deadly poison' (Jas. 3:4–8). In these striking words James describes both the importance of the tongue and the terrible havoc in human relationships caused by failure to discipline 'the unruly member'. His observations are amply confirmed by experience; and the evil caused by gossip, destructive criticism and idle words, enable us to understand our Lord's severe statement: 'that men will have to give account on the day of judgement for every careless word they have spoken. For by your words you will be acquitted, and by your words you will be condemned' (Matt. 12:36, 37). 'No man can tame the tongue' (Jas. 3:8), but God can tame it, and this is a most important aspect of Christian discipline all too lightly ignored by many Christians. Several ways may be suggested of establishing this discipline, and of co-operating with God in answering the prayer: 'Set a guard over my mouth, O Lord; keep watch over the door of my lips' (Ps. 141:3).

One of the most effective ways to do this is to make a habit of thinking before speaking. How often we have 'let slip' words we would do anything to recall, 'careless words', because of a failure to observe this rule. There are three questions we might habitually ask of any of our utterances—is it true? is it kind? is it necessary?

Is it true? One ought never, of course, to say anything which is not true; yet how often false impressions can be given by exaggeration, by distortion, by withholding all the facts, by half quoting and other departures from strict honesty of word. Accuracy in speech is more difficult than is commonly supposed, but it can be attained with practice. In this respect we need especially to be on guard when speaking of those we do not naturally 'like'.

Is it kind? One of the greatest evils of the tongue is the negative and destructive criticism of others *in their absence*. This can be eliminated altogether by observing a simple rule such as the following—'I will not say in anyone's absence anything I would be unwilling to say in his presence'. There is a place for constructive criticism—but that should always be made privately to the person concerned, and not to others in his absence.

Is it necessary? Words are precious things, and we are warned again and again in the Bible about the dangers of too much speech. Mr. Talkative is *not* among the King's pilgrims on the way to the celestial city. Of course, this last test should not be applied too strictly—that would be absurd—but it is probably true to say that most of us talk far too much, and listen too little. All these suggestions are finely summed up in Paul's great phrase 'speaking the truth in love' (Eph. 4:15).

4—Time

Great inequalities of wealth exist among men, and yet there is one respect in which all are equal—God gives to us all each day the same amount of *time*. We are responsible to God for the manner in which we use that time. We all need to learn—to quote the title of a book by Arnold Bennett—'How to live on twenty-four hours a day'. The right use of all our time is put first on the list in the famous 'Consecration Hymn' of Frances Ridley Havergal—'Take my moments and my days, let them flow in ceaseless praise'; for if God has all our time he already has almost everything. How then shall we rightly use our time?

To begin with, it is an excellent thing to keep a diary—not the kind which is written up at the end of every day, recording the events that have already happened, but a book in which we write all our future engagements. In this way it is possible to plan future commitments, and to present all our time from being consumed in a whirl of activities. This is the real temptation of the Christian nowadays, quite as much as that of sloth or laziness. Modern life is so hectic that without careful planning it readily degenerates into a rushing here and there to no real purpose. The coinage of time may be wasted through laziness—it is more likely to be wasted because we are busy doing nothing!

A diary is an excellent device for keeping a check on oneself, and for preventing a multiplicity of activities. With the aid of a diary it is possible to plan out the coming week, and Sunday usually provides an excellent opportunity to do this. It will be found that there are certain unavoidable commitments each week, arising out of one's responsibilities in the home, at work, as a citizen, and as a member of the church (see chapter 8 on 'Service'). When these obligations have been given their due place, the Christian will learn to carry them out in an ordered manner, irrespective of his moods or feelings at the time. If, for example, he is due at 'evening classes' on Wednesday, and 'Bible study' at church on Thursday, he will not be deflected from his plan merely because it is raining, or there is a good programme on the television!

In this connection, isn't it a disgrace that so much of our Christian service and church attendance should be dependent upon the weather, or some other accidental circumstance? Such an attitude towards our daily work would never be tolerated. Planning (and sensible loyalty to such plans) is the answer to the tyranny of moods and interruptions. In this plan of the week, it is of course necessary to set aside time for recreation, leisure and social life; apart from these any person will become tired and stale, and a Christian can still hear the Lord saying, 'Come with me by yourselves to a quiet place and get some rest' (Mark 6:31).

The planning of each day is no less important than the planning of the longer periods, for here, too, it is true that 'whoever can be trusted with very little can also be trusted with much' (Luke 16:10). But here we are much helped by the necessities of life itself, for the bulk of the day is already planned for us by our fixed hours of work. There will be a need, however, to plan 'our own time' before and after the fixed hours of work. 'Before'—it will be necessary to discipline oneself to get up at the appointed hour at the (horrid!) voice of the alarm-clock, and to set aside adequate time for morning prayer. There is no need for advice about setting aside adequate time for breakfast! (The reader is referred to chapter 2 on 'Prayer' for a fuller treatment of this important point.) The period *after* work hours will normally be spent according to the weekly diary already referred to, and should always include time for evening prayers. Never forget to take care of the odd moments, and the larger periods will take care of themselves. Journeys may be usefully employed in reading, short periods for writing a letter or other odd jobs. In many such small, as well as in larger, ways we learn to 'use the present opportunity to the full' (Eph. 5:16, NEB).

5—Spending money

The whole of our money and all our possessions belong to God, and are to be used as he directs in his service. The Christian cannot rightly say 'mine' in any absolute sense; he is the steward who must give an account to his Master for the way in which he uses his goods. This principle of stewardship of money and possessions is of the greatest importance, and in practice involves the following points in the modern world.

In the first place, the Christian must learn to live within his income. Mr. Micawber's advice still holds good: 'Annual income twenty pounds, annual expenditure nineteen nineteen six, result happiness. Annual income twenty pounds, annual expenditure twenty pounds ought and six, result misery.' This may be hard advice for people with small incomes, but it is a necessary discipline if we are to 'let no debt remain outstanding' (Rom. 13:8).

It is an excellent thing to budget all money, and that for several reasons. It helps to keep a check on our expenditure, and enables us to see at a glance whether we are living within our income.

It reveals how our money is being spent, and thus enables us to cut out unnecessary or extravagant spending. But, chiefly, it helps us to plan the spending of our money, and this is the most necessary thing of all.

While there is a place for giving on impulse or in response to special appeals, it is advisable to plan in advance for expenditure of our money. The Christian will, first of all, decide how much to give to the Lord, putting aside a weekly sum for the work of the local church, and giving this whether or not present every Sunday. Today most churches issue envelopes for weekly giving. Money should also be given for missionary work and for the needy people of the world—whether it is given to and through one's own church or directly to the cause concerned. The essential thing is that this giving should be regular and ordered, and not left to whims and passing impulses.

Then we must allocate money for other necessary expenses, running the home, expenses relating to work and other such commitments. In these matters there may appear little to distinguish the Christian from the non-Christian, but the former should think carefully and prayerfully about his standard of living and especially his spending on luxuries. These are not necessarily wrong, but nor, especially in an age of enormous worldwide poverty, are they our automatic right. The right use of God's money does not, of course, exclude expenditure on recreation and other personal things; these will be given their due place in the planning of our spending.

As Christians we should also act as stewards of our possessions, using them all to the utmost in the service of God. We can use our houses and gardens to offer the hospitality encouraged in the New Testament. Our cars can be at the disposal of God, especially in offering lifts to the elderly. We should be willing to lend any of our goods if they can help others (Matt. 5:42). The Christian can at this point set a good example, and witness to a possessive and money-worshipping age, as when it was said of the early Christians that 'no one claimed that any of his possessions was *his own*' (Acts 4:32).

6—Mastering the body

Since 'the Word became flesh and lived for a while among us', we have learnt to honour the body which 'is a temple of the Holy Spirit, who is in you' (1 Cor. 6:19). This shrine of the Holy Spirit must be kept pure and holy, and devoted entirely to the service of Christ. We must pray with Jeremy Taylor: 'Let my body be a servant of my spirit, and both body and spirit servants of Jesus.' 'Brother Ass the body' is, however, often a most rebellious and unruly servant, and like Paul we need to 'master' it, bringing it into complete subjection. By careful training and discipline the body can become a fine instrument of the spirit of man, and of the Spirit of Christ.

It will be the aim of the Christian to possess, as far as possible, a healthy body for the service of God and man, and everything possible should be done to achieve this objective. Recreation, fresh air, outdoor exercise and sport, are important. Daily physical exercises and other excellent (and now plentiful) devices for 'keeping fit' are to be recommended. To have a well-trained body is by no means unconnected with the spiritual life.

The final gift of the Holy Spirit mentioned by the apostle Paul is 'self-mastery' or 'self-control' (Gal. 5:23). The Christian must take possession of this gift by exercising discipline over the body. The desires of our lower nature should not be permitted to take control, however pressing and urgent: every impulse and desire should be controlled, brought into subjection to Christ.

Remembering that laziness is the root of many other sins, we will learn to get up every morning at the fixed and right time, and will refuse to laze and lounge about during the day. The 'sins of the table' are little spoken of nowadays, but they are none the less real. Gluttony in eating or drinking is a sin against the body, and against the Holy Spirit.

Needless to say, there must be firm control of the powerful sexual impulse; this must begin with discipline of thought-life and imagination, for at this point the inner life of desire and the outer life of action are closely related.

It is important that the body should not be despised or treated as a disreputable relative; it is a creation of God, and all its instincts and impulses may be used in his service. It isn't possible to control what we refuse to accept, and self-control implies self-acceptance. The Christian is not called to be an emaciated hermit seeking to stifle and root out all bodily impulses. We should accept, control, use, direct and consecrate all our bodily, mental and spiritual powers in the Master's service.

In conclusion, two points must be mentioned: one by way of warning, one of encouragement. Many people fail to live a disciplined life, not because they don't make the attempt, but because it's not an all-round attempt. It is useless to concentrate on one part of life and to ignore another—indiscipline in any part of life adversely affects the whole.

The word of encouragement is this: the establishment of

discipline is a slow process, which cannot be achieved in the twinkling of an eye or by waving the magic wand of pious resolution. An athlete becomes such by constant training. 'In all matters referring to the ordering of conduct, it is little use to make abstract and general resolutions of improvement. The practical way of bringing about improvement is by constant little acts of the will, carried into effect' (*The Obedience of a Christian Man*, Dickie).

Let us never forget that the Christian is called to be 'a good soldier of Christ Jesus', to show in character and conduct all the qualities of a good soldier. Now, no one can carry out the suggestions here made without the military virtues of courage, endurance, obedience and discipline. The Captain of our salvation himself calls us to leave behind soft, indulgent and spineless living. 'Take your share of suffering as a good soldier of Christ Jesus.' The Christian soldier will not fail to do this, having a powerful motive and a steady aim—'to please his commanding officer' (2 Tim. 2:3, 4).

Questions

1. If salvation is all of God's grace, what is meant by the statement 'Work out your own salvation'?
2. Is it possible to have too much discipline in the Christian life?
3. Discuss the connection between 'discipline' and 'discipleship'.
4. Why is the Bible so severe on the sins of the tongue, and how are such sins best avoided?
5. Make out a rough plan of how you can best spend your time:
   (a) tomorrow, (b) next week, (c) through the coming year.
6. 'Give an account of your stewardship.' Reply personally to this order.
7. 'Let my body be a servant of my spirit.' In what ways can this be brought about?

5.

How to Deal with Temptation

THIS CHAPTER TELLS YOU

It is not wrong to be tempted; the sin is in yielding to temptation.

1. *Mental alertness and prayer are both necessary if temptation is to be overcome.*

2. *The dangers of a merely negative goodness.*

3. *There are various stages in temptation. The place where evil should be dealt with.*

4. *How to deal with the problem of a besetting sin.*

5. *The importance, when tempted, of directing the attention to the Saviour.*

6. *The Lord Jesus has already gained the victory for us on the cross. How this victory may become ours.*

'You can't help birds flying over your head, but you can prevent them from building their nests in your hair!' This graphic saying expresses two facts about temptation: that everyone will be tempted, but that such temptation can be resisted and overcome. As we shall be concerned in this chapter almost entirely with the latter truth, we may begin with a word about the former. Temptation is a universal experience; no member of the human race is exempt from it. 'All have sinned' (Rom. 3:23) necessarily implies that 'all have been tempted'—and all *will* be tempted, for 'things that cause people to sin are bound to come' (Luke 17:1). No man then is in a position to choose whether he will be tempted or not. It follows from this that it cannot be wrong to be tempted; that which is 'bound to come' cannot be our moral responsibility. It is wrong to *yield* to temptation; but it is not wrong to be tempted. It is necessary to grasp this important distinction. Our Lord himself was severely tempted, not only at the beginning but throughout his ministry (Matt. 16:23; 22:18; Luke 22:28), yet he was entirely without sin. We too shall be tempted, and must expect it, for 'to be forewarned is to be forearmed'; but we can overcome temptation through him 'who has been tempted in every way, *just as we are*—yet was without sin' (Heb. 4:15), for 'it is as he suffered by his temptations that he is able to help the tempted' (Heb. 2:18, Moffatt). How then can we overcome?

1—Watch and pray

'Watch and pray so that you will not fall into temptation' (Mark 14:38). In this and other similar sayings (cf. Mark 13:33, 37) the Master impresses upon us the need for constant watchfulness and mental alertness if we are to overcome temptation. The apostles underline and develop his teaching on this point. 'So then, let us not be like others, who are asleep, but let us be alert and self-controlled' (1 Thess. 5:6). 'Be self-controlled and alert. Your enemy the devil prowls around like a roaring lion looking for someone to devour' (1 Peter 5:8). In the latter quotation the apostle Peter gives the reason why such watchfulness is needed. In the same way the apostle Paul warns us against 'the devil's schemes', giving this as the reason why the Christian should put on 'the full armour of God' (Eph. 6:11). Because the devil is so crafty, subtle and clever, frequently disguising himself as 'an angel of light' (2 Cor. 11:14), the disciples must be fully alert and able to say 'we are not unaware of his schemes' (2 Cor. 2:11).

It is a very great mistake to underestimate the strength and subtlety of an enemy in physical or military conflicts 'against flesh and blood'; how much more foolish then to relax our alertness against 'the powers of this dark world'. Many people fall victims to temptation just because they have become too 'cocksure' and self-confident, not realising that this is itself a subtle temptation. 'So, if you think you are standing firm, be careful that you don't fall!' (1 Cor. 10:12). The solemn words of Christ, although originally spoken with reference to his advent in glory, are capable of a much wider application: 'What I say to you, I say to everyone: "Watch!"' (Mark 13:37).

'. . . and *pray*'; here again the Lord himself is our example, for in the darkest hour of trial in Gethsemane, he first told the three apostles to pray, and then turned to prayer himself. So also in 'the Lord's Prayer' we are taught to ask 'deliver us from the evil one', and the Saviour himself prayed for Peter that he might be victorious when 'sifted' (or tested) by Satan (Luke 22:31). For it is in prayer that we receive the strength and grace of God to overcome temptation, and whenever we 'lift up holy hands in prayer' our spiritual enemy is defeated, as when Moses on the hill defeated Amalek with the uplifted hands of intercession (Exod. 17:11). It is very important, however, in prayer, *not* to concentrate the attention upon sin. The mind should be stayed upon God, and the attention directed in prayer to the *positive* grace or virtues needed, and not upon the sins one wishes to overcome. It is always wrong to concentrate upon sin. To take one particular example, do not pray, 'O Lord, deliver me from my bad temper', but rather 'O Lord, give me your Holy Spirit, and especially his fruits of patience, self-control, and peace.' The rule is, concentrate in prayer upon the positive graces or virtues you need, and not upon the vices or faults you wish to overcome.

2—The empty house

'When an evil spirit comes out of a man, it goes through arid places seeking rest and does not find it. Then it says, "I will return to the house I left." When it arrives, it finds the house unoccupied, swept clean and put in order. Then it goes and takes with it seven other spirits more wicked than itself, and they go in and live there. And the final condition of that man is worse than the first.' (Matt. 12:43–45.) In this description of the house of the human heart which has undergone a spring-cleaning and is subsequently left *clean* but *empty*, the Saviour depicts for us the dangers of a merely negative goodness. Unless a man invites new tenants into his house, the old demon will return—with seven others. Some of our Lord's contemporaries had repented at the preaching of John the Baptist, and had cast out certain evils from their lives, but they had refused to respond positively to the Saviour by inviting him into their empty 'reformed' hearts, nor had they responded with enthusiasm to his purpose. Their 'goodness' was merely negative and temporary; and their last state would be worse than the first.

It is a fact that the empty life will inevitably be taken over by sin. Evil can never be driven out by a direct and sustained attempt to exclude it; evil is driven out only by taking in the good, by what is called 'the expulsive power of a new affection'. Now many people are engaged in a constant and tiring struggle to drive out the 'demons', and often wonder why they meet with so little success. They are attempting to be *good—for nothing!* The same energy should be diverted to the *positive* task of filling the house of the heart with good tenants, so that when the 'demons' peep in at the windows they will find it full and occupied. What does it mean to fill the house? Just this—invite in the Lord Jesus Christ, and let your life be fired with the 'new affection' of love for him; seek the companionship of his disciples, make good friends, and enjoy real, satisfying fellowship. Throw yourself with energy and enthusiasm into his work, making the kingdom your dominating purpose; spend time each day in prayer, Bible reading and meditation—in a word, let *all* your powers be fully engaged in the worship and service of the Lord Jesus Christ. Set out to be good *for* something; be positive. 'No heart is pure which is not passionate, no virtue is safe which is not enthusiastic' (Sir John Seeley). Many people are led into evil just because some part of

47

their nature is crying out for positive, creative expression. We are not intended merely to exist like cabbages, but to have life to the full as sons of God. In allegiance to our Lord every part of our nature can find full and harmonious expression. The immediate answer to temptation must be a 'No', but the ultimate answer to all temptation is a 'Yes' to the Lord Jesus who leads us into abundant life.

3—Toying with temptation

Once upon a time a camel-driver was asleep in his tent in the desert on a bitterly cold night. In the middle of the night he woke up to find that his camel had pushed its nose beneath the flap of the tent, and he was about to protest when he realised that only a very little of the camel was inside, so that it didn't matter much. On waking up later, however, he found that the camel had inserted its whole head and long hairy neck into the tent. The man now roused himself from his lethargy to protest, but the camel prevented him by saying, 'Oh, do you really mind? It's so terribly cold outside, and I won't come in any farther.' The man consequently went off to sleep again, but on waking the third time he was really alarmed to see that the camel's front legs and hump were now in the tent. As he was about to leap to his feet and drive it out, the camel said again, 'Now I solemnly promise this time that I won't come in another single inch—and besides, it's warmer for you in the tent if there are two of us inside.' The man was so lazy that, in spite of the growing apprehension in his mind, he fell off to sleep again. Very soon, however, he awoke with a cry of terror, 'Help!', for he found the heavy weight of the camel on top of him. 'If it's room you want,' said the beast in answer to his cry, 'there is plenty of room outside—get out!'

Sin, like the camel, doesn't walk right into the tent of a man's life; if it attempted to do that, we should repel it at once. Sin worms its way in by gradual stages. The man had no intention of allowing the camel to take possession of the tent; but the beast did so, because he dallied with it, instead of decisively repelling it. Now sin gets hold of us in temptation in four quite distinct phases. First of all an evil *thought* enters into the mind (this is the camel's nose), and if it isn't at once repelled it passes into the second stage of *imagination* —that is, we begin to picture ourselves doing the evil thing (the camel's head and neck). To picture evil, however, awakens and rouses the *desire* to do evil (the camel's legs and hump), and this in turn impels us towards the evil *action*. What then is the right way to deal with temptation? No man can help evil thoughts entering into his head—everyone has them, which is only another way of saying that we are all tempted. But we can all prevent evil thoughts from passing over into evil imaginations and desires. 'You can't help birds flying over your head, but you can prevent them from building their nests in your hair!' The rule is, therefore, always deal with temptation when it first comes in the realm of thought, and never dally with it. Deal with the camel when he first puts his nose beneath the flap of the tent, for you will find it most difficult to deal with him at the later stages. Don't play with temptation.

4—That besetting sin

Many Christians find themselves constantly hindered by one particular sin which causes them to stumble again and again, and which in popular speech is usually referred to as 'the besetting sin'. (That is not the true meaning of the phrase in Heb. 12:1, KJV.) For such people, the moral struggle seems to be centred upon that one particular point. First of all it should be pointed out that it is foolish to concentrate upon any one sin. This is often the main cause of the difficulty. At the risk of being misunderstood we would suggest that God himself is much less interested in that 'besetting sin' than we are. Human nature is evil, but God's purpose is to make us entirely good through his Son, and it is with the transformation of our *whole* nature by the Holy Spirit that God is concerned, not the lopping off of particular faults or vices. It is possible to resist the transformation of our whole nature by redeeming grace by concentrating upon tidying up the character at certain points, and leaving it essentially unchanged. The Christian must, then, co-operate with the Holy Spirit in an all-round discipline, and avoid any tendency to focus on a few selected faults or 'sins'. A strongly fortified position held by the enemy is not usually captured by frontal attack, but by outflanking movements; if a discipline is steadily applied to the whole of life, one particular point will soon have to 'fall into line'. The rule is, then, 'practise self-restraint all round', and do not give all your attention to one particular thing.

Another reason for frequently repeated failures has already been suggested in section 2, entitled 'The empty house'—the failure to accept and use in a right and positive way the strong instincts, impulses and desires inherent in our human nature. Now none of the instincts and emotions of our nature is evil in itself, but only becomes corrupted and evil when directed to wrong ends. The same material can be directed to right ends in the service of God and man. Paul was a born fighter, but he did not use that pugnacity to hit his neighbour in the eye. He used and directed it in fighting 'the good fight'. We too can use all there is in us in a right way, and then it will not erupt like a volcano in a wrong and destructive way. And finally it must be realised that discipline can never be achieved at any point merely by waving the magic wand of magnificent resolution—but only by constantly carrying into effect little practical acts of self-discipline. Self-mastery is given and achieved under the authority of the Master in the same way that the athlete gains his strength and skill—by constant practice.

5—Fixing our eyes on Jesus

We now turn to a very practical point. We are all tempted; what then should we do in the actual moment of temptation? We have already stressed the importance of dealing with temptation when it first comes, but how in fact should we deal with it? One thing is very clear—it is a great mistake to concentrate upon the evil thing which is tempting us, in order to fight it. Experience shows that this is exactly what many do—with fatal results. The way to overcome temptation is not to fight evil, for in order to fight evil the attention has to be concentrated upon it, and the more we concentrate upon fighting evil within ourselves, the more we shall be enslaved by it. Many people fail to overcome temptation, not because they don't try, but because they try too much—in the wrong way.

The right thing to do is to redirect the attention, to look elsewhere, and that for the Christian means to 'fix our eyes on Jesus' (Heb. 12:2). 'The true function of the will is the direction of the attention', and when the mind is turned to Jesus, evil loses its appeal, and we are reinforced with his grace and power. It is fatal to all true spiritual progress to be preoccupied with oneself, especially with one's own temptations. Such a way does not lead to life and victory, but to morbid obsession with evil and self-absorption. Rather, in times of temptation, we must establish the discipline of looking away from self to our Redeemer in his holiness and power. The Christian athlete throws off 'everything that hinders and the sin that so easily entangles' him by fixing his eyes on Jesus (Heb. 12:1, 2).

6—Victory through the cross

We have just stressed the point that the attention must be redirected in temptation from the evil thing to Christ the Saviour. But why to him rather than anywhere else? This takes us to the heart of the gospel. 'Christ died for our sins'—it is just these five words which make all the difference to the way in which the Christian must face sin and temptation. Calvary was a battlefield, and there our Lord fought with all the hosts of darkness on the cross, and 'made a public spectacle of them, triumphing over them by the cross' (Col. 2:15).

On the cross, Christ won a complete victory, a decisive triumph. The powers of evil have been defeated and overthrown; 'the strife is past, the battle done'. A decisive military victory may often have to be followed by 'mopping up' operations, to deal with the remaining enemy forces. But that continuing campaign is influenced by, depends upon, and is the outworking of, the victory already won. The soldiers of Christ are still engaged in warfare, but it's a fight with a difference. We struggle to enter into full possession of the victory of Christ already won. The reason for our defeats is that we do not believe, we do not receive, we do not trust. Receive the Saviour, trust in his redeeming blood, live in him by faith and obedience, look to him at all times of temptation—and sin will have no more dominion over you. For 'this is the victory that has overcome the world, even our faith' (1 John 5:4).

According to an Indian legend, a massive Hindu warrior once went into battle and fought with a ferocity and vigour that no one could resist, killing masses of the enemy. Eventually, however, he met with one stronger than himself, and in the ensuing struggle his head was cut off. But so strenuously was he fighting that even when his head was cut off his body went on dealing out blows. In this way he killed several more soldiers, until at last someone shouted to him—'Look, your head's off!' At that he collapsed in death.

The head of sin has been cut off on Calvary by the 'strong Son of God', but the monster goes on injuring and killing people because they don't tell him so. Sin has no power, except to unbelief. On the battlefield of temptation, the Christian, like the emperor Constantine, must lift up his eyes to the cross and see in letters of fire the words, 'In this sign conquer.'

Questions

1. *'The harder I try to conquer this particular sin, the more I seem to fail.' What advice would you give to such a person?*
2. *How would you deal with the problem of impure thoughts?*
3. *What are some of the chief 'schemes' of the Devil?*
4. *How can a Christian prepare himself in advance to resist future temptations?*
5. *'The Lord Jesus has overcome sin; we have but to rest in his victory.' What are the practical implications of this true statement?*
6. *What is the underlying disease of which all our so-called 'sins' are symptoms? How may this disease be cured?*
7. *In what different ways does the Lord Jesus help us in our warfare against evil?*

6.
How to
Receive Guidance

THIS CHAPTER TELLS YOU

1. *The guidance of God should be the normal experience of every Christian.*

2. *The kind of language in which God conveys his messages to us.*

3. *Guidance comes to us through different media, such as the Bible, the church fellowship, wise and trustworthy friends, and the circumstances and events of life.*

4. *Sometimes guidance is received through direct impulses of the Holy Spirit. How to test such impulses. The place of conscience and common sense.*

5. *How to come to a decision when in perplexity over a specific problem.*

6. *The goal is to possess 'the mind of Christ' in everything.*

1—The promise

Should every Christian expect to receive the guidance of God? If so, in what ways is such guidance given? Before we go on to discuss the practical answers to this latter question, we ought to begin by reminding ourselves of the divine promises. The guidance provided for the children of Israel in their wilderness journeyings was unmistakable; they had the pillar of fire by night and the cloud by day. The word of God to the Psalmist was equally distinct: 'I will instruct you and teach you in the way you should go; I will counsel you and watch over you' (Ps. 32:8). In the New Testament we have the words of our Lord himself: 'when he, the Spirit of truth, comes, he will guide you into all truth . . . he will tell you what is yet to come' (John 16:13). The subsequent experiences of the early believers in the Acts of the Apostles show that the guidance of God was a necessity expected and a blessing continually enjoyed. Action was taken as 'it seemed good to the Holy Spirit'.

We must begin, then, with the confidence that guidance is not something unusual, exclusive to a privileged minority of Christians. It is one of the 'all things' that make up the inheritance of those who belong to Christ. If we love him, we should expect his guidance. The Christian life is a direct, personal relationship with God. As we live in the enjoyment of this relationship we shall take pleasure in speaking to him, and we shall also listen while he speaks to us. The former is prayer: the latter includes guidance.

2—How God speaks

We understand quite clearly what it means to speak to God. Every time we pray, although there is no physical form that we can see, we believe and know that God is listening and waiting to answer. It is when we think of this communion in the reverse direction that problems begin to present themselves. We speak with words to express our thoughts and desires. How does God speak? The answer is, that he does not use audible words, but uses the language of inner conviction implanted by the Holy Spirit.

The Holy Spirit is our teacher. The thoughts and messages through which God is seeking to guide us are implanted by the Holy Spirit in the form of deep personal conviction.

Examples will make this more clear. 'When he comes, he will convict the world of guilt in regard to sin and righteousness and judgement' (John 16:8). When the Spirit implants a conviction of sin; he is acting as *judge*. In the same chapter, in verse 13, the promise is given that he 'will guide you into all truth'. In this case he is acting as *guide*. He may do this by implanting a conviction concerning some Christian truth or positive duty. In every case it is God speaking to us through the Spirit. We shall proceed in a moment to indicate some of the practical channels which the Spirit uses to implant these convictions, but for the moment it is important to emphasise that we should be ready to recognise the voice of God.

Two further observations may be necessary at this stage. The first is that we need to train ourselves to receive and recognise these promptings of the Spirit; this will involve waiting upon the Lord, without which progress is not possible in any part of the Christian life. The second is that we should not be disturbed or disappointed at not hearing any audible voice or at the lack of 'gusts of feeling' or 'luminous thoughts'. We shall have learnt that God speaks in other ways.

3—The means God uses

We now come to a consideration of the ways in which God speaks to his people. These are some of the channels along which guidance comes to us, leading to those inner convictions we have already discussed. In the era before Christ, God appointed definite channels—there was the temple, also the priests and the prophets. An interesting list of some of the methods of guidance God used in the Old Testament is given in 1 Sam. 28:6: Saul 'enquired of the Lord, but the Lord did not answer him by dreams or Urim or prophets.' What are the channels God uses under the new covenant? In other words, *where* do we go to 'enquire of the Lord'?

(a) *The Bible.* God has revealed his ways and purposes in the

Bible. We do not come to the word of God to cover as much ground in as short a time as possible; if we read it aright, it will be in the spirit of, 'Speak, Lord, for your servant is listening.' The Bible will be the means of implanting convictions of sin and positive duty, and it will then be our responsibility to act upon those convictions.

It is important also to notice that from scripture we do not receive only particular guidance for some immediate need; more especially we come to a general knowledge of God's will and purpose. Without this, it is hardly possible to make any decision aright. We can therefore regard our Bible reading as supplying the *framework* for all guidance. This point is brought out in the answer Jesus gave to the Sadducees: 'You are in error because you do not know the Scriptures' (Matt. 22:29).

Many of our problems concerning guidance would be solved if we would check up our actions against the principles clearly laid down in the book which reveals God's will and purpose in Jesus Christ. Simply stated, God does not supply guidance in some more personal way contrary to truths he has already revealed in scripture. Whose fault is it if we find difficulty in reaching a friend's house, all because we have neglected to read the letter containing travelling instructions that our friend sent to us? Instructions for the journey from earth to heaven have already been given in outline in God's word, the Bible.

(b) *The Christian Fellowship.* The church is 'the fellowship of the Holy Spirit', and if believers live together in mutual love the Spirit will give guidance through the fellowship which he has created and made his dwelling-place. This he will do in the first place through teaching what is written in the Bible. In the public reading of the Bible and through the preaching and teaching from it, God 'speaks' to those who approach him in worship, giving practical instructions.

Again, God speaks through the fellowship in prayer and conference. When, in Acts 13:2, the Holy Spirit 'said' to the church at Antioch, 'Set apart for me Barnabas and Saul for the work to which I have called them', how do we suppose that voice came to them? Was it an audible voice? Might it not have been in a manner similar to the way the Holy Spirit sends a man out into the ministry or mission field today, by implanting a conviction in all hearts as the church meets for discussion and prayer? There is a tremendous value in the guidance that comes when praying people meet together in Christian fellowship to 'enquire of the Lord'.

(c) *The Advice of Others.* This is in some respects an elaboration of the previous thought. God may guide through the advice of other Christians more advanced in the faith. It is not often wise to ignore the help of those who have greater experience, wisdom and consecration. There is probably somebody in your church or among your acquaintances to whom you feel you could go for this kind of help. For example, Paul's first letter to the Corinthians was written partly in reply to certain specific questions the church had sent to him. The Christians needed guidance on matters that were perplexing them, so they consulted Paul. This underlines an important New Testament principle, that God speaks to people through people. We ought to have a high regard for the advice of wise pastors and other mature Christians—while recognising, of course, that none is infallible and that we must ultimately look to God for the revelation of his will in his word and by his Spirit.

(d) *The Circumstances of our Life.* The Holy Spirit may use the outward circumstances of life to guide us. A door of opportunity may clearly be opened before us; or, negatively, the shutting of a door may equally clearly settle a problem. The account of Paul's journeyings in Acts 16:6–10 illustrates this kind of guidance. There was an experience of the Spirit preventing the missionaries from preaching in certain places; God was leading them on into Europe, hence the vision calling them to 'Come over to Macedonia and help us', and their 'concluding that God had called us to preach the gospel to them'. A day quietly committed to God may well mean that the Spirit will indicate his guidance through a friend, a book or a conversation. We must never dissociate the 'guidance of circumstances' from the other promptings already mentioned, but the opening and shutting of 'doors' are seen to be among the movements of the Spirit as we grow in our understanding of the mind of Christ.

4—Impulses and how to test them

(a) *Direct Impulses of the Holy Spirit.* We have dealt with four ways in which the Holy Spirit guides us, and in every case he uses some medium, such as the Bible or a Christian friend. He does not, however, restrict himself to these channels. Sometimes the Christian has a direct, unpremeditated impulse to do something, and the heart in tune with Christ recognises this impulse as the message of the Spirit. For example, reference to Acts 8:26–39 will show that Philip was guided in this way when he was used in the conversion of the Ethiopian eunuch. Again, in the story of Hudson Taylor's conversion we are told of his mother's 'impulse' to pray for her son at the crucial moment—although she was miles away and without information of his movements at that particular moment. Books on personal work often include many such examples of impulsive guidance of this kind. Such experiences light up the pages of the New Testament, and happen today. We must be ready for this kind of guidance, and the best preparation will be a humble spirit and a devoted heart. Of course, it is wise to test the 'impulses' we receive by all available standards, especially conscience and the Bible. 'Test the spirits to see whether they are from God' (1 John 4:1).

(b) *Conscience and Common Sense.* Never despise the place that should be given both to conscience and to common sense. All people have an inner moral sense, an awareness of right and wrong (Rom. 2:14, 15). It is hardly necessary to concern ourselves with other forms of guidance when conscience clearly tells us that a certain action is wrong. We do not kneel down to ask God whether it is right for us to steal! Again, sanctified common sense is a very precious part of the Christian's equipment, and will deliver us from making many foolish mistakes. Faith transcends reason, but does not render it useless. Blessed indeed are those who possess common sense in uncommon measure.

We must be careful of what has been called the 'blank mind'. The Bible does not appear to support the view that if we make our minds a blank and 'listen to God' he will reveal his will in such a way that plans for the day can be taken down in detail. We have indicated the main biblical truths concerning guidance already.

We ought therefore to be suspicious of any suggested 'methods' that by-pass fundamental biblical principles; there are no short cuts to guidance, any more than there are to salvation or holiness.

People with impulsive temperaments will need to be particularly watchful. Damage can be caused by too hasty action that all too glibly claims the blessing of God. The various ways of checking guidance already indicated will be sufficient, if closely followed, to avoid these unfortunate happenings. It is only necessary here to point out the danger. Humility is necessary in this as in all other parts of the Christian life. A humble, teachable mind will counteract the dangers of an over-impulsive temperament; such a person will not be too dogmatic, especially in early years, about matters which are generally regarded as controversial. It is a comforting thought, however, to remember that God does overrule our mistakes, and many a blunder made in our blindness and sin is taken up in his gracious providence and turned into something good.

5—Guidance in perplexity

Guidance is needed by the Christian in two ways. Unless we distinguish the two, there is bound to be confusion. General guidance relates to the whole of life. The disciple wants to be assured that the whole plan of his life is unfolding under the gracious control of God. But there is also a need for particular guidance. The time comes when advice is needed for a specific course of action. A decision must be made within a very short time. *How* is one to know God's will? We will, therefore, take the principles already given and apply them to a particular problem. A difficult decision has to be made, or a problem resolved. What does one do?

(1) Begin with *prayer*. Tell God all about your difficulty, in detail, and ask for his guidance. Remain in the spirit of prayer, which means that he keeps in close touch with you, and you with him all the time.

(2) *Think* out the whole matter as far as you are able. This means that you should use all the information available, as well as

employ all your faculties to the utmost. The use of the reason must not be regarded as an unspiritual aid. God gave us our minds, and he intends us to use them. We are not to regard guidance as a crude and mechanical substitute for our own mental effort. The wonder and beauty of God's guidance is seen partly in the fact that he goes *beyond* the best that human judgement and common sense can attempt. These other things are not to be despised, they are to be exercised in the Christian life by supernatural help.

(3) Having prayed and thought, the next step is to *ask the advice* of a wise and trusted Christian friend. This friend will not know the details of the case as well as you do, but he may well be acquainted with the workings of God's Spirit in similar matters. You may be fortunate enough to have a small group of friends that you can thoroughly trust with your difficulty. Talk your problem over with them. But, remember, none of this advice is to be regarded as final. The Holy Spirit may use a number of channels, and you are to act as a result of all the aids that have been given to you, not any one of them.

(4) While you are waiting, and deciding, do your *immediate tasks* faithfully and well. If we are sincere in claiming that we want to do God's will in a matter that is causing us some perplexity, then plainly we must show it by doing his will in smaller and more obvious matters nearer at hand. 'Whoever is faithful in small matters will be faithful in large ones' (Luke 16:10, GNB). To cite just one example, a young man who is puzzled as to whether God is calling him to be a missionary or evangelist is not to spend all his time puzzling, but rather working hard for the kingdom of God in his own church and neighbourhood. It is a biblical principle, and a very important one to emphasise just here, that God gives further guidance only as we act in obedience upon that which has already been received.

(5) It may eventually be found that the Spirit gives a *gentle urge* in a certain direction. Perhaps a door opens (or closes); or there is a steadily deepening inner conviction about the right course of action to be taken. This will prove sufficient to indicate the next step. As that step is taken, the way will gradually, step by step,

open out. There will be an increasing sense of confidence, until we are able to see the truth of the apparently puzzling statement so often made, that 'guidance is easier to see when we look back than when we look forward.'

(6) At some point in this sequence a *definite* decision must be made. We are seeking the mind and will of God, but we come to a point where we ourselves must 'make up our mind'. This is probably what is meant in Acts 16:10 when the writer declares: 'we got ready at once to leave for Macedonia, *concluding* that God had called us'. There had to come a time when the missionaries 'concluded' something. When you have made your decision, act upon it, and do not reconsider it. Trust in God and his grace to see you right through. It is possible that you may not fully realise how definitely you were guided until much later on.

6—The mind of Christ

Guidance is such an intimate part of the whole Christian life that it must not be separated from the other aspects of life with which this book is concerned. The chapters on prayer, Bible reading, personal discipline and guidance, form a unity. The guided Christian is the praying Christian; just as discipline is necessary for those who would obtain the greatest spiritual enrichment from Bible reading.

This brings us to what is undoubtedly the most important truth concerning the guidance of the believer. As we go on with him the mind of Christ is formed in us; we think about things his way and make decisions as he would make them. We recognise the influence that living with a person has upon our thoughts and actions. Our Lord Jesus, by his Spirit, lives *in* us. As the Spirit is allowed to have control, he will form in us the mind of Christ, until it is Christ within us making the decisions and directing the life. We must make this our aim. Then we shall be able to say with Paul: 'I have been crucified with Christ and I no longer live, but Christ lives in me'(Gal. 2:20). 'We have the mind of Christ' (1 Cor. 2:16).

Questions

1. *What are the principal means God uses to guide us?*
2. *What would you do if the advice of your friends conflicted with your own convictions?*
3. *Is conscience infallible?*
4. *You have been offered an important new post and must give your decision within twenty-four hours. What would you do?*
5. *Why is common sense not enough when making decisions?*
6. *'Speak, Lord, for your servant is listening.' What do you expect to happen as a result of such a prayer?*
7. *Discuss the use, and misuse, of the Bible in guidance.*

7.

How to Live in Fellowship

THIS CHAPTER TELLS YOU

1. *That the Lord Jesus came, not to save a number of individuals, but to create a new community.*

2. *The reasons why you should belong to a local church.*

3. *Personal qualities of character which are essential if Christians are to live successfully together.*

4. *There are various circles of fellowship, such as the world-wide church, the local church and 'the church within the church'. How to enjoy fellowship at its best.*

5. *The kind of programme suitable for a small Christian fellowship.*

1—All one in Christ Jesus

The story of Robinson Crusoe is a thrilling account of the kind of life a resourceful human being can lead for a considerable time in complete isolation. Robinson Crusoe Christians, however, are just not possible; for Christian fellowship is not an optional extra, but is an essential part of the Christian life. To be a Christian is to share the common life of the Body of Christ.

The early chapters of the Acts of the Apostles clearly and attractively portray the life of the first Christian community. '*All* the believers were *together* and had everything in common' (Acts 2:44). They prayed together, worked together, and even shared their possessions. The Holy Spirit who had come in great power upon them had created 'the fellowship of the Holy Spirit', and had shown himself to all in the joy and power of a shared life, a common life, a community life.

The Lord Jesus had himself taught his disciples that they were related to him as branches to the vine; because of their common relationship to the vine, the branches are in relationship with one another. The life they received from Christ was the life they themselves shared. They could only remain in him, the true vine, by obeying his new commandment: 'love each other as I have loved you'. Here the Master teaches us that our relationship with him is inseparable from our relationship with one another, and later prays that they may 'be brought to *complete unity* to let the world know that you sent me' (John 17:23). The world will not be convinced of the truth of the gospel until his disciples are 'all together' in the unity of faith and love. The apostles develop this teaching of the Master, expressing the same truth in other graphic ways. Christians are 'living stones' built *together* on the foundation of the apostles and prophets to be a new temple, a 'dwelling' lived in by the Spirit (Eph. 2:19–22; 1 Pet. 2:5). They are all members of the Body of Christ, 'joined and held together' (Eph. 4:16), and 'the eye cannot say to the hand, "I don't need you"' (see 1 Cor. 12:12–31). Christians are to be related as intimately as are the different members of the human organism. This unity of believers in Christ is symbolised best in the fellowship meal, the Communion, in which 'we, who are many, are one body, for we all partake of the one loaf' (1 Cor. 10:17).

The New Testament knows nothing of the solitary Christian, and the apostles would have regarded a statement such as 'I believe in keeping myself to myself' as incompatible with the

Christian way of life. To reject 'togetherness' is to reject Christ, for we cannot be reconciled to God through him without at the same time being reconciled to one another. God's purpose is 'to bring all things in heaven and on earth together under one head, even Christ' (Eph. 1:10). It is not the salvation of a number, even a very large number, of isolated individuals, but the creation of a new community, a holy nation, a royal priesthood—the church. Fellowship therefore is not just a part of the Christian life; it *is* the Christian life.

2—Why meet together?

Now if Christians are to be 'all together', which is God's purpose, then they must meet together; and this gathering together of Christians in one locality is the local church. The local church is the universal church in that particular place, e.g. 'the church of God which is Corinth' (1 Cor. 1:2, GNB). The best definition of a church is to be found in the words of our Lord, 'where two or three come together in my name, there am I with them' (Matt. 18:20). The real presence of Christ is promised to believers gathered together in his name, and it was to the whole fellowship that he made the similar promise, 'surely I will be with you always'. We meet together in Christ's name because there supremely we meet Christ, and this is the chief reason why we should 'not give up meeting together...but... encourage one another' (Heb. 10:25).

Nowadays there are many people who profess—in a vague and nebulous way—to belong to the church universal, but do not attach themselves to any local church. Such a position is illogical, and shows a very defective knowledge of God's purpose in Christ. Is it possible to be in the Army without belonging to any particular unit in it? What would be said to a potential sailor who said: 'I am keen to belong to the Navy, but I firmly refuse to be put on any particular ship!' We belong to the whole church triumphant in heaven, militant on earth, *through* the local church, and we belong to it because 'togetherness' is God's will and purpose.

Now Christians gather together in accordance with God's will for three main reasons:

(a) *To worship together*. The Christian fellowship has been created to worship God. We are 'being built into a spiritual house . . . offering spiritual sacrifice acceptable to God'. The worship which is acceptable to God is corporate worship, the offering of a redeemed community made one by faith with its head, Jesus Christ. Even when the believer worships in the quiet and solitude of his own room, he is worshipping 'with all the redeemed' as a member of the community of Christ. Such worship finds its highest expression in the service significantly called 'Holy Communion', the family meal, which is at once fellowship with God and with one another through Christ. So also the purpose of preaching and Bible teaching is to build up the fellowship (not 'me' as a solitary individual), which is built up 'to offer up' spiritual worship. The church then is primarily a worshipping community.

A responsible Christian will then, unless unavoidably prevented, always be present when his fellow-believers gather together for worship; and not only on Sundays but also on the more informal occasions when the fellowship meets for prayer. Whether such meetings are held in the home, at work, or in the church building, particular blessings belong to such prayer (see Matt. 18:19).

(b) *For mutual help*. Christians are all members of Christ, and therefore all members one of another. The members of the human body are all inter-dependent and complementary; so, too, Christians need one another. They are to edify or build one another up in love. One of the most beautiful Greek words in the New Testament is *philadelphia,* denoting the warm affection, the brotherly love which pervaded the early communities. They were so obedient to Christ's commandment of mutual love that even a pagan was moved to exclaim, 'See how these Christians love one another!'

Christians help one another most by sharing their knowledge and experience of Christ. So Paul writes to Philemon, 'By their participation in your loyal faith they may have a vivid sense of how much good we Christians can attain' (v.6, Moffatt).

Christ is not our private possession, but our common-wealth, and we are to share him. John Wesley wrote concerning the 'Holy Club' at Oxford, when God was preparing the early Methodists for the great work they were afterwards to do, that they made known to one another the real condition of their heart. Personal testimony, the sharing of experience, is an important aspect of Christian fellowship. It does not mean telling everybody everything always; but it does mean a willingness, as directed by the Spirit, to tell our fellow-Christians of our triumphs, our temptations, our problems, and sometimes of our faults and sins. 'Therefore confess your sins to each other and pray for each other so that you may be healed' (Jas. 5:16). If we have wronged the fellowship in any way, we should confess and seek the forgiveness of our fellow-members.

But of course, sharing Christ means much more than this—something positive. We are to share our knowledge of him and of our faith, and this is best done in the Bible study group. Fellowship around the Bible, especially when each member of the group makes some contribution, is deeply enriching. Through our rich and varied heritage of psalms, hymns, prayers and devotional writings we share the experience of those who have gone before us; so, too, by our corporate study in a discussion circle of contemporary books on the Christian faith and life, we can participate in the knowledge and experience of the church universal today. There must also be a sharing of material wealth and possessions with those in need; apart from this, Christian fellowship will be 'up in the air' and lacking in practical expression. As this question of stewardship has already been dealt with (in the chapter on 'Discipline'), no more need be written here on this subject.

(c) *For service together.* A few thousand soldiers fighting as individual units would lead to hopeless confusion in time of battle. These same men united and welded together into one striking force would constitute a factor to be reckoned with. Christians 'joined and held together' constitute the church, the 'body of Christ', and this is the organism through which Christ does his work in the world. This does *not* mean of course that the church can work only when and where Christians are gathered together. A loyal Christian in a factory is doing church work, for he is there as a member of the fellowship with its plans and strategy behind him. A paratrooper may be dropped by himself in enemy territory, but he is part of an army, and is acting upon the army's plan. 'Lonewolf' Christians (if the contradiction may be allowed) are of very little value to the work of the kingdom, because so often such work has no survival value, being unrelated to the main plan of the Captain. This plan is to make known *'through the church,* the manifold wisdom of God' (Eph. 3:10). The various ways in which the church may serve others are set out in detail in chapter 8.

3—How to live together

Christian fellowship is a creation of the Holy Spirit, but as we have already stressed (in chapter 1 and chapter 4), he works through human obedience and co-operation. Such fellowship is not therefore automatic, and may in fact be marred and even destroyed by human disobedience. This sometimes happened even in the apostolic age (much of 2 Corinthians is about this), and today our sins against Christian unity, love and fellowship are too glaring and obvious to need pointing out. It is therefore the responsibility of every Christian to 'make every effort to keep the unity of the Spirit through the bond of peace' (Eph. 4:3). As the apostle here says, we cannot just take fellowship for granted; we must make 'every effort', take great care, assume personal responsibility, for the building up of the fellowship in truth, unity, peace and love. We must, then, go on to ask what qualities are needed in the believer if there is to be unity and love in the fellowship. Apart from these qualities, however imperfectly developed, any believer can be a disruptive influence, 'a spanner in the works'.

There is in fact one quality needed, and that is *agape,* the love of Jesus in us. Love is the spirit of the Christian community, the mortar which binds together all the living stones of the new temple. But this love is not a sentimental quality, nor is it merely emotional. It reveals itself in many sterling qualities essential in community life, and in the New Testament these aspects of *agape* are called 'the fruit (not fruits, for they are all aspects of one quality) of the Spirit' (see Gal. 5:22, 23). They are love, joy, peace, patience, kindness, goodness, faithfulness, gentleness, self-control. These are the virtues of life in community (compare Col. 3:12–17; Phil. 2:1–5; Eph. 4:25–32; Rom. 12). We intend now not to give another list, but to single out a few of the main qualities implicit in these New Testament passages.

(1) *Loyalty*. One of the chief qualities required of husband and wife within the marriage covenant is faithfulness. Now Christians have entered together into a covenant, the new covenant, made by the sacrificial death of Christ; the love between them is covenanted love, faithful love. Mutual loyalty is the primary thing in Christian love; we who share the same loaf and drink of the common cup must be utterly loyal to one another. This applies especially to the tongue; never gossip about fellow-Christians, or speak disloyally of the church before non-Christians (see chapter 4:3).

(2) *Candour*. The fellowship is built up by 'speaking the truth in love'. Both words in this inspired phrase are essential. All fellowship is founded upon mutual trust, and this is possible only as members of the fellowship speak the truth to one another. Truth clears away all suspicion, and the health of the body of Christ depends upon it. But it must be spoken 'in love'. We are to be truthful and tactful, honest and constructive, candid and kind. The Master himself was frank in his utterances, yet he was never unloving.

(3) *Responsibility*. The Body of Christ is frequently rendered impotent because so many of its members are not functioning, but are mere passengers—more like parasites. To take responsibility, to be active instead of merely passive, denotes maturity. Assume responsibility for the welfare of your fellowship, and don't just leave it to others.

(4) *Co-operation*. The success of a football team depends in a large measure upon co-operation amongst its eleven members; a church to be successful must be a team, a co-operative society.

There must be a willingness to work in harmony with others, even if it means abandoning one's own pet ideas or personal peculiarities. 'If I can't have my way, then . . .'—such an attitude is disloyalty to Christ. There are sure to be differences of opinion and viewpoint in any company, and co-operation often depends upon a creative compromise. Try to see any truth on the other side when a difference arises; learn to distinguish between essential and unessential things; be charitable even when you cannot agree, and always remember the wise saying, 'Think it possible that you may be mistaken.' Humility is essential: 'Do nothing out of selfish ambition or vain conceit, but in humility consider others better than yourselves' (Phil. 2:3).

(5) *Patience and forgiveness*. The church is not a fellowship of perfected saints, but of forgiven sinners; our fellow-believers are all imperfect, and are sure at times to try our patience. There will be folk in the fellowship who will irritate us; others whose peculiarities annoy us; some we do not 'like'. Hence the need for self-control, for patience, for forgiveness, for 'bearing with one another in love'. It is a good thing to remember that we too probably annoy other people and they have to make allowances for us. Try to appreciate the difficulties of others, due, perhaps, to temperament; pray for those you do not like, and seek if possible to help them. Avoid small-mindedness and pettiness as unworthy of 'the grace of the Lord Jesus Christ'. Remember that he taught us to pray, 'Forgive us . . . *as* we forgive.'

(6) *Humour*. Joy is inconceivable apart from a certain gaiety and lightness of heart, that playful irony which is so evident in many of the sayings and parables of Jesus. A sense of humour is essential for life in fellowship, for apart from this we are sure to suffer from distorted vision, and carry quite needless burdens. It is a sign of real grace to be able to laugh with others, and it is a sure sign of maturity to be able to laugh with them *at* yourself. There is no need to take *everything* seriously, and the Creator gave us humour for that very reason.

4—Circles of fellowship

When a stone is thrown into a still pond the ripples move outwards in ever-widening circles. This is a picture of Christian fellowship, which may be visualised in the form of a number of circles falling within one another, i.e. concentric circles.

The outermost circle is the church universal, which not only includes all believers now living upon earth, but also those who have died—all the faithful in Christ Jesus in heaven and on earth. It is a great inspiration to remember that we are 'surrounded by such a great cloud of witnesses', and to realise that the living and the departed are in one unbroken fellowship, 'the communion of saints'. Intercession for the world-wide church upon earth—for her unity, for the purity of her faith and the success of her work—should have a prominent place in the prayer-life of every believer.

By *the outer circle* we mean the local church or assembly of believers, which falls within the universal church. It is here that the believer probably first encountered the Lord in the Bible and the fellowship and here one must learn the meaning of life in community. No amount of ordinary human geniality or social activity will make such a church a fellowship in the spiritual sense, but only a common allegiance to Christ and unity in his worship and work.

The inner circle is found within every local church and has been called 'the church within the church'. Even within Israel there was a faithful remnant, and 'those who feared the Lord talked with each other' (Mal. 3:16). It consists of all those who are committed, those who accept responsibility, the reliable workers. They are usually dissatisfied with things as they are, and are always ready to take action to bring about changes. If it is objected that there ought not to be such a group within a local church, since all should be zealous—we agree; we are describing things as they actually are.

The innermost circle is not found by every Christian. With one or two others, at the most very few, there may be relationships of intimate personal knowledge and complete mutual trust centred in Christ. Ideally this should exist in a Christian family between

71

husband and wife; such families were often the nuclei around which churches were formed in the days of the apostles. Such an intimacy of fellowship may be enjoyed by close friends united in Christ in a common faith, love and purpose.

We may compare the fellowship in the days of our Lord's ministry. There was the outermost circle of all his disciples, the outer circle of the twelve apostles, the inner circle of Peter, James and John, and finally 'the disciple whom Jesus loved'. But the point to be stressed is this: all these circles fall *within* one another. That is to say, all Christian fellowship is inclusive and not exclusive. It is hardly possible to exaggerate the importance of this. An exclusive 'fellowship' is a clique, and is in fact a denial of the common life in Christ. It is not actually possible or even desirable that one should enjoy the same depth and intimacy of fellowship with everyone, but our deeper experiences of fellowship should give us something more to contribute to the wider circles.

This outline of the circles of fellowship will suggest an important principle: move towards the centre, pass through the outer courts to the inner shrine. And the centre of all Christian fellowship is Christ. As with the spokes of a wheel, we cannot approach the hub without approaching one another, and the closer we approach one another the nearer we are coming to the hub.

5—A plan of action

In chapter 8 of this book we shall describe in detail some of the ways in which a Christian may serve the outer circle, his local church, and through it the outermost circle of the universal church. We are concerned now with the inner and innermost circles—that is, with small groups, or teams, or cells of Christians in very intimate relationship. Those who are eager to spread the kingdom should come together in this way, whether in the home, or place of work, or in the local church. The communists have much to teach us about the effective working of such cells. The definition of a Christian given in the opening chapter might be taken as the basis for membership, and we conclude by giving an outline of the suggested activity of such a group.

(1) *Prayer:* in this activity the real unity of the group is realised and its life sustained. It should include the worship of God, petition for the members of the group, and intercession for others.

(2) *Silence:* in the fellowship of silence the whole group can 'centre down' upon God and seek the guidance of the Holy Spirit. It is a good thing when discussing questions or plans to give periods of time for quiet thought, meditation and waiting on the Holy Spirit. Don't be afraid of plenty of silences.

(3) *Sharing of experience:* in confidence, the members of the fellowship share with each other 'the real condition of the heart', confessing failures, sharing difficulties, problems, experiences, plans, and successes. This is the road to mutual knowledge and help.

(4) *Study:* group study of the Bible may take place either by members sharing the truths discovered in personal reading (each member doing the same daily readings), or by the study of a passage together, sharing all thoughts that come out of it. The same may be done with other selected Christian books.

(5) *Personal evangelism:* the group should seek to expand by winning others. Some time should be spent planning the next steps, in seeking guidance on whom to approach, in planning individual and corporate evangelistic action.

(6) *Service:* a group should attempt to discover ways in which its members personally or together may be of service to others— the relief of need, visiting the sick or lonely, social action; any job that needs doing.

(7) *Hospitality:* using the home as a base, a cell can do excellent work for the Kingdom through hospitality. This may mean having a dinner or supper-party to establish contact with out- siders, or having a coffee-evening, during which witness is made.

(8) *Daily work:* a group should think out the way in which the new life must affect the daily work of each of the members and seek to apply the conclusions.

(9) *Church:* a cell should attempt to discover what contribution it may make to the life of the local church, and be an available team to do any jobs there.

We may fitly conclude this chapter on fellowship by drawing attention to a petition which is a part of 'the high-priestly prayer' which Christ offered up 'on the night he was betrayed'. This is the Master's prayer, not for them *but for us*. 'My prayer is not for them alone. I pray also for those who will believe in me through their message, that all of them may be one, Father, just as you are in me and I am in you. May they also be in us so that the world may believe that you have sent me' (John 17:20, 21).

The Lord Jesus asks that the perfect unity between the Father and the Son may be reproduced in the personal relationships of believers, so that the world, seeing that unity in love, might believe. This prayer is of great significance. The church will convince the unbelieving world by the very quality of her own fellowship, and all men will know that we are his disciples, and that 'He came from God', when we love one another. Let us all co-operate to fulfil this prayer of our saviour, and by the quality of our mutual love, fellowship and unity, compel the unbeliever *in our own age* to exclaim, not in sarcasm but in wonder, 'See how these Christians love one another!'

Questions

1. '*My religion is a personal matter between God and myself.*' Discuss this statement.
2. What evidence can you discover in the Gospels that the purpose of the Lord Jesus was the creation of a new community?
3. If fellowship is an essential of the Christian life, what happens to a Christian who is forcibly deprived of it? (e.g., a soldier in the army or a missionary in a remote heathen village).
4. '*I can be just as good a Christian without going to church.*' Is this assertion true?
5. What are the main functions of the Christian church?
6. '*I am very shy and reserved and find it difficult to mix with others.*' How would you advise such a Christian?
7. Is there any difference between fellowship and friendship?

74

8.
How to Serve God

THIS CHAPTER TELLS YOU

1. *To examine your equipment for service. How you can find out what you are best fitted to do.*

2. *How to use your home in the service of God.*

3. *How to make your job a part of Christian service.*

4. *Your duties as a citizen of the nation.*

5. *How to be an active, useful member of your church; some of the jobs you can find to do in the church.*

6. *All work can be service of God.*

The pen is made for writing, and the sword for fighting; the soldier is trained for battle, and the apprentice for his trade. What then is the purpose behind the creation and training of Christian character? Now while true Christian character is always attractive and beautiful, yet it is not created merely for ornamental purposes; it is meant for use, for service. We are saved to serve; and service for the Master involves the service of our fellow-men. In what ways then can we serve him?

We shall attempt to answer this question now, but let us first be quite clear about the full Christian meaning of the word 'service'. It is so loosely used today—almost any commercial concern, for example, offers us 'service'—that we need to go back to the perfect example. Our Lord was a servant and his life reveals the meaning of service. He gave himself without reserve to others, a self-giving that reached its climax on Calvary. Service was not one activity of his life, it was his whole way of life, and 'whoever says that he remains in union with God should live *just as Jesus did*' (1 John 2:6, GNB). 'For even the Son of Man did not come to be served, but to serve, and to give his life as a ransom for many' (Mark 10:45). For the Christian, the life of Jesus Christ is the dictionary which defines the word 'service'. No other definition is required. While never losing sight of our example, we must now concern ourselves with the practical problem of how we may best serve him in our day and particular situation. Assuming that we have a real desire to be of some use to the Master—just *what* can we do, and *how* can we do it? We will deal with the questions in that order.

1—My equipment

A soldier is not sent out to fight with his bare hands; he is equipped for battle. God does not expect us to serve him without any equipment. But we are not all fitted out in exactly the same way. The surgeon in the hospital theatre, the shorthand-typist in her office, the radio operator in the plane, the farmer on his combine-harvester—each is equipped with different instruments and endowed with various skills. In the parable of the talents (Matt. 25:14–30) all the servants *received something* with which to serve, although they received differing amounts. We too have *all* received 'talents' from God, and they constitute our equipment or service. By 'talents' are meant natural gifts, abilities, aptitudes for doing certain things. For example, John has a gift for public speaking, Jack is good at youth work, Fred is handy with tools of all kinds, while his brother Tom is a born athlete; Mary has a musical talent, whereas her sister Jane simply loves nursing in hospital. The list might be continued almost indefinitely, but, although there is such variety, they are all gifts, and the Giver intends them to be used in his service. Take stock then of *your* equipment. What are your talents?—for obviously that will indicate to you your special line of service.

The best way you can set about finding the answer to this question is by asking two others: 'What are the things which I do really well?' and 'What are the things I really *enjoy* doing?' In this connection we need to be on our guard against two mistakes. The first is that of a false modesty which says, 'Oh, I don't really possess any special gifts'; that simply isn't true, for 'to each one the manifestation of the Spirit is given for the common good' (1 Cor. 12:7).

This is often an excuse for fear or laziness, and is an accusation against God; it is 'buried talent' attitude. The other mistake is to attempt forms of service for which we are not suited, and in which we become just 'a square peg in a round hole'. This, no less than laziness, may hinder God's work. Find out your real talents, and then you will be able to tackle a job for which you are equipped, and do it well and successfully. Remember too that many of our gifts are latent and need to be developed and cultivated. As was stressed in the introductory chapter, gifts need to be practised in order to be possessed. There is one talent, or more probably there are a number of them, however insignificant they may appear to you, which God has given you for his service. Accept this fact now; do not be mock-modest about your capabilities.

Our gifts or talents tell us *what* we can do; we turn now to the next consideration, where and how are we to use our equipment? This brings us to the main spheres of service, of which there are four in number—my home, my job, my country, my church.

2—My home

'Charity begins at home.' This familiar saying is true also of service. That is where Jesus first learned to serve. It is tackling things in the wrong order to begin by looking far afield for opportunities of service while ignoring those close at hand. For this reason some Christians who are well spoken of in society are not so popular at home. Being a Christian should make an immediate difference to the quality of our family life. It is important to realise that grace, courtesy, good temper, helpfulness and service are needed *more,* and not less, if we are to live the Christian life with those we know so well. The Christian will assume responsibility to build up home-life, and will avoid the modern tendency to treat home merely as a restaurant and a dormitory. Lend a helping hand in the housework, and don't leave all domestic duties to an overworked wife or mother. The quality of our discipleship is often (rightly) judged by such little things.

Service in the home, however, means much more than this, for every Christian home can be made a vital cell in the work of the kingdom of God. The home of Aquila and Priscilla, whether it was at Corinth, Ephesus or Rome, became a church of Christ, a contagious centre of Christian life and fellowship. This can be accomplished in the first place through the wise practice of hospitality. John is a young man whom you wish to influence and win for Christ; ask him home to tea, or for supper in the evening, and perhaps introduce him to Alan, a Christian friend. Mary, although a Christian, hasn't many friends and makes no progress in her spiritual life; invite her to your next party and help her to get to know other Christians. The home is the finest of all places for getting to know strangers and for establishing relations of friendship, an essential preliminary in evangelism. It is an admirable piece of service, in particular, to invite non-Christian friends to tea on Sunday, and then take them along with you to hear the word of God at your church.

The home may also be used for larger gatherings, and it is a fact of experience that it is much easier to get a friendly and informal atmosphere in a home than anywhere else. A party may begin with the usual games and fun, and be followed after supper by a well-prepared session at which personal testimony is given. A coffee-evening to which every Christian brings along a non-Christian guest, and where a suitable talk is given, has been a means whereby many have entered the kingdom. Furthermore, such a home soon establishes a reputation for friendliness and hospitality; folk in need come to know that there they can find help and encouragement. It is a fact that the church outside the house can never rise above the spiritual level of the church in the house, and the fellowship and expansion of the former depends to some extent on the latter.

3—My job

It is significant that a person's job should often be referred to as his or her 'calling'. That is what it should be, for our daily work is intended to be a vocation given us by God. A Christian should be conscious of a call not only to the ministry—but to every ministry, whether it be teaching, medicine, law, agriculture, politics or road-sweeping. One of the greatest needs of modern society is the restoration of a sense of God's calling to man's daily work; every Christian worker can help towards this.

To begin with, very great care should be taken in choosing one's career, in order to make certain that what we choose is God's calling. If it can be avoided (this is not always possible) a Christian should not just drift into any job that turns up, or that offers the biggest wage at that particular moment. The choice of a job should be made a matter of earnest prayer, and the advice of others should be sought (see chapter on 'Guidance'). Here above all else it is necessary to ask: 'What are my talents?', 'How can I best serve God and my fellow-men?' Vocational guidance and advice can be obtained today, and it is often possible to get specialised training. Unfortunately it may be much harder to find a job. The Christian who finds himself unable to secure paid employment may be able to use some of the time in working for the church or in the local community.

A Christian should aim at being a good worker. 'Work hard and do not be lazy. Serve the Lord with a heart full of devotion' (Rom. 12:11, GNB). If Christians are incompetent or inefficient, the world is not likely to be impressed. It is for us to introduce a new motive into daily work; we are not to work with our eyes on the clock for so much a week; we are to work 'as serving the Lord'. All work done for his sake is part of the service of God.

In addition to this there are many other ways of serving God's kingdom through our daily work. The Christians working together in one place should get together to discover what they can do together in that situation. For example, those working in a large factory can form a cell in that factory, to work there for the kingdom; such a cell can not only encourage each member in his personal witness, but can also accomplish something collectively —perhaps arrange a service in the canteen or a film in the concert hall. Why leave it to the communists to provide striking examples of the success of such 'cells'? In the case of Christians working in a large city those working in the same profession (e.g. police, lawyers, doctors) can sometimes join together and such unions can more readily reach their fellow-workers. If there is a Fellowship or Christian Union where you work, should you not join it? Christians meeting in prayer and discussion groups can think out and apply Christian principles to their own job, and perhaps take corporate action to correct abuses and help others. If such things were done on a large scale, less would be heard of the criticism that some Christians serve Christ on Sundays and Mammon throughout the week; 'no one can serve two masters'.

4—My country

A Christian is a citizen of two kingdoms, and has responsibilities to both—Jesus taught us to 'give to Caesar what is Caesars's, and to God what is God's' (Mark 12:17). The civil order is an institution of God for the establishment and execution of justice (Rom. 13:1–7), and it is the responsibility of the believer to help in this task. We are called to be the salt which prevents the world from becoming totally corrupt. In proclaiming the gospel in word and life, the Christian is a true patriot, since 'righteousness exalts a nation' (Prov. 14:34). There are, however, other ways in which he may serve the civil order.

Christians should consider taking up careers that would enable them to exert the maximum influence upon society in general. For example, the work of a Christian school teacher can be a mighty influence for good, and the churches should be producing a constant stream of them. In the same way we need more—far more—Christian politicians, magistrates, welfare officers, social workers, etc. In this way the influence of the Lord Christ is brought directly to bear upon the social order, and there is hardly any job, however humble, which he cannot use in this way.

Christians should also take responsibility in their local government, a sphere of service very much neglected. If numbers of committed Christians were on their County, District or Parish Councils, they could use their influence not only negatively against certain social evils, but positively in such important matters as education, youth work, housing, etc. Christians should be the conscience of society, with deep concern, like that of the Old Testament prophets, for what is right in society.

This, of course, must include an intelligent interest in national affairs. Christians are not justified in ignoring such matters; they should be concerned with the welfare of all their fellow-citizens. Christians should be involved in the struggle against war, poverty, bad housing, unemployment—in a word, against all that is contrary to the spirit of Christ. If it is said that this is not church work, we reply that all work done by a member of the church is church work, and all true service of our fellow-men is service of God.

5—My church

All believers are members of the Body of Christ and, as in the case of the human body, every member has some function to perform. It is said that the only member of the human organism which has no function is the appendix, a notorious source of trouble—which is a parable! And yet how many Christians are content to remain 'passengers' in the church of Christ, content to enjoy the services and accept all the privileges, while always avoiding the responsibilities. It's an unpleasant thought, but there are many parasites in the Body of Christ, living on the organism to which they never contribute a thing. If this is so, then it is plainly a state of affairs that the Christian disciple must avoid. How then can we serve the church and, through the church, the kingdom of God?

At this stage it is important to distinguish between two aspects of service in the church: there are some functions which are common to all Christians, but there are also others which require a special gift. Under the former heading there are:

(a) *Worship*. The church has been created for the glory of God,

81

and worship should be her chief and constant activity. Every believer as a priest of Jesus Christ has the responsibility of offering up these 'spiritual sacrifices' (1 Peter 2:5) both in his private prayer and in the corporate worship of the church. There can be no acceptable service of the church apart from regular, common worship, and the first answer to the question frequently asked, 'What can I do to serve the church?' is 'Take your proper place in its worship.'

(b) *Intercession*, on behalf of the church and other people—of all types. This unites us still further with our exalted Lord, who 'always lives to intercede' for us. Intercession is work; it is service which often achieves more than a good deal of (merely) human activity. Pray for the preaching of the word (especially on Sundays), for all church officers and members, for the church universal and for the salvation of unbelievers. Join with others in this intercession if there is a weekly meeting for prayer in your church. Prayer may be the only form of service possible for invalids, the infirm and the aged, whose question is often, 'What can I possibly do for the church?' Find out from your minister or sick-visitor the names of people for whom you may intercede, and regard this as your special contribution to the work of God. 'More things are wrought by prayer than this world dreams of' (Tennyson).

(c) *Building up*. In the New Testament, Christians are urged to 'build each other up' (e.g. 1 Thess. 5:11), by showing loving interest in other members, and a concern for their spiritual welfare and material needs. Each is to be concerned for the well-being of the others in the fellowship (Phil. 2:4), and thus the community will be built up in love. It is 'the fellowship of the Holy Spirit'. In practice this means that each member must get to know as many of the other members as possible, always trying to encourage and strengthen the faith of others, and to help them when they are in need. Every Christian can show the spirit of love and warm fellowship. No church is strong without this. (See chapter on 'Fellowship'.)

(d) *Witness*. It is the responsibility of every church member to bear personal witness, both by life and word, to the gospel of

Jesus Christ, and to take some part in the evangelisation of the world. Apart from those kinds of evangelism (mentioned below) which require special gifts, there are at least three main ways in which all Christians can witness: through friendship and personal work as described in chapter 9, through bringing other people to hear the gospel at church (see section 2 of this chapter), and through generous support of missionary work both at home and overseas.

We turn now to the consideration of those types of services in the church which require a special gift—although, as we have already observed, gifts are often latent and need cultivating. We should not be too quick to conclude that we are not suited for a special piece of work, for Christ can often develop our gifts if we are willing. This list is not of course exhaustive, but is intended to stimulate the reader to explore other avenues of service.

(1) The preaching of the word, or the gift of public speaking. Here there are possibilities of service not only for the ordained minister, but also for the lay preacher, and especially for the person who is willing to give addresses, not necessarily at public worship, but to youth meetings or other departments of the church. There is a constant demand for this type of service, usually far in excess of the supply.

(2) The work of teaching is a gift not to be confused with the above. It may be the teaching of Primary children or Juniors, or the running of a Bible class or study group for the young people. The Sunday School and youth departments of any church normally require many such teachers, and nowadays valuable teaching aids in the form of notes and lesson outlines are always obtainable.

(3) Leadership in youth work is a valuable, if exacting, sphere of service, and is of importance. The youth leadership of our churches should be as proficient and as well trained as that of secular youth movements. If that goal is to be achieved the right type of leader, and proper training, will be necessary. Many Christians could render fine service in the Boys' Brigade, the Scouts, the Guides, the Girls' Brigade, the Young People's Fellowship, the Covenanters, the Campaigners, or whatever particular organisation is attached to the local church. Normally,

of course, such openings are available chiefly to those within the organisation concerned.

(4) If elected by the church, a Christian should serve in the various offices of the fellowship, whether as Elder, Deacon, Church-warden, Steward, Secretary, Treasurer, Superintendent, etc., and take part in the government of the church.

(5) A church visitor can make a valuable contribution by visiting the sick and needy, encouraging those in any kind of trouble, keeping in touch with all church members, and those whose membership has lapsed. There should be several such workers in every church, acting together in fellowship with the pastor as joint shepherds of the flock.

(6) Going from door to door with literature requires a certain amount of courage and tact, but it is an excellent way of contacting outsiders (especially children), and provides many opportunities for witness. This type of work can be tackled systematically by a team.

(7) Open-air work, if it is well organised and carried on in a suitable place, can be a valuable form of evangelism. A strong team of workers, good music and singing, and powerful and interesting speakers are needed. This is essentially a joint effort requiring a combination of gifts.

(8) Much more use could be made in the church of the gift of journalism, by writing suitable articles for the church magazine or for the local press, or in the preparation and distribution of special leaflets. A church should also have a book-stall for the sale of Christian books and pamphlets, and should maintain a supply of the latter for free distribution. All those who are interested in books, literature and writing can find suitable openings for service in these directions.

(9) Music and song can serve the gospel, and if you have a good singing voice it can be used in solo or choral work. If you play any instrument, that too may be used in the service of God.

(10) Skilled hands will find many ways of rendering service to the church. The builder, the carpenter, the plumber and the sign-writer all have their contribution to make.

(11) Finally, it is important that every church member should

be generally useful, available and 'handy'. There are all kinds of jobs defying any classification which need to be done in odd places at odd moments; they are usually left to the faithful few. A person who is on the alert, ready and willing, will always find plenty of opportunities for service, however humble, for Christ and the church.

6—'Your spiritual worship'

Our service to God and his kingdom should ideally include all four spheres: the home, daily work, the country, the church. It is all 'God's service'. It is wrong to think that there are two types of work, secular and religious, and that the service of Christ is concerned with the latter only. Such an error introduces a false division into life which inevitably develops into an attempt to 'serve two masters'. Work on a Monday morning is as Christian as work on a Sunday morning, if both are done 'for the Lord'. 'If'—that is the whole point, for it depends on the motive behind all our work and service. William Law in his justly famous book, *A Serious Call to a Devout and Holy Life,* coins a phrase which sums up the whole meaning of holiness in daily living—'the intention to please God in all our actions'. It is that simple motive which, when present, transforms all service into service for God, and transfigures the common task with the light of his glory.

Questions

1. *'But there's nothing I can do in the church.' How would you reply to such a statement?*
2. *How can we discover the talents that God has given to us?*
3. *Discuss the ways in which your home could be used for the service of God.*
4. *'A Christian should leave politics severely alone.' Is this the true Christian attitude?*
5. *What contribution could be made to the service of the church by (a) an invalid, (b) a footballer, (c) a commercial traveller, (d) a journalist, (e) a housewife?*
6. *Should any distinction be made between sacred and secular work?*
7. *What is the greatest possible service that can be given to another person?*

9.

How to Lead Others to Christ

THIS CHAPTER TELLS YOU

1. *That making disciples, like fishing, is an art which can be learned.*
   The qualifications required by the personal worker.
   Some of the reasons why we fail to do this work.

2. *The first task is to win the confidence of the other person; five stages by which this may be done.*

3. *The second phase is to lead the other person to Christ; the five further stages involved in doing this.*

1—Fishing for men

When our Lord Jesus Christ called Peter and Andrew to be his disciples, he did so with the words, 'Come, follow me...and I will make you fishers of men' (Matt. 4:19). In calling them, the Master had a definite job for them to do—they were to leave off fishing in the sea of Galilee for work of a similar kind. 'From now on you will be catching men' (Luke 5:10, GNB). In common with Peter, Andrew and the rest of the apostles, we have been called to follow Christ in order to share in the same purpose. The command and commission of him to whom all authority has been given in heaven and on earth is, 'Go and *make disciples* of all nations'

(Matt. 28:18, 19). This is the word of the Lord Jesus to every believer, and great are the joys of, and the promises made to, those engaged in this work. When, however, the Lord Jesus called his disciples from catching fish to catching men, he did not assume that they already knew how to make disciples. He said, 'Come... and I will make you fishers of men.' Fishing is an art which must be learnt; already they had learned how to fish with nets in Galilee; now they were to learn, from watching the Master himself at work, how to catch men. We must stress the truth that fishing is a skill and there are effective ways of doing it. When salmon fishing, for example, one does not march up to a river, throw in a brick, sling in a bent pin on the end of a piece of string baited with a page from a fisherman's manual, and invite a salmon to be caught! One can, of course, do just that, and subsequently console oneself by relating stories of the large salmon one nearly caught! Bringing others to Christ is an art to be learnt, a skill to be acquired. This chapter assumes that the reader already has some desire to help others come to Christ, and proceeds to outline some ways of setting about it.

Before we look at these, two warnings are necessary. First of all, it is important to make clear the fact that men cannot be won for Christ merely by using a particular method: it depends on the person using it. And the necessary qualifications of the personal worker are as simple as they are searching: a real love for the Lord Jesus Christ and a real love for ordinary men and women. Paul's words are supremely true in this context; 'but if I have no love, I make nothing of it' (1 Cor. 13:3, Moffatt). Love, the controlling love of Jesus, is the all-important reality in this work, and method is quite secondary. It is not, however, unimportant, and there is a need both for the motive power of love and wise, tactful method. If we really love the men and women for whom Christ died, we shall be eager to know how to win them, and in that case technique itself becomes an expression of love.

Why do we so often fail to do this work? One of the chief reasons is because we have little love. In fact, there should be here no distinction between eagerness and love. The only way to get this love is to pray for it and then act on the assumption that you have it: you will find, in action, that you have. Love will overcome all the other many obstacles which hold us back from this work. What are these? First, there is laziness; and the cure is action, definite and practical action. Then there is natural timidity and reserve, especially the fear of receiving rebuffs. This may be due to pride or to temperament, or to both; the cure is to do habitually the thing of which you are afraid. The young preacher may often feel afraid when facing a congregation—but he doesn't bolt! It should be added that for most of us there will probably always be a shrinking back from this work; it would be dangerous if we didn't feel like that about it. There is also a natural fear of making mistakes; but 'the man who never makes mistakes never makes anything'.

Finally, we may refrain because we do not feel 'fit' to do it. We may feel ignorant of the Bible and the Christian faith; we may feel morally unworthy, conscious of compromise in our own life; we may feel incompetent—'I do not know how to speak; I am only a child.' Of course we are not 'fit', but mercifully our task is not to point to ourselves, but to Jesus as Lord. If we wait until we are 'fit', the world will perish. But of course we must allow the Spirit to make us more fit—and the only way to cure ignorance of the Bible is to study; the only way to speak effectively is to practise, the only way to abolish moral compromise is to consecrate our-selves and live obediently. Remember, Jesus has said, 'I will make you fishers of men.'

2—Friendship

If we are to lead anyone into a committed relationship with Christ as Lord and Saviour we must first win their friendship and confidence. We shall now discuss some ways of building the sort of friendship which can lead to the opportunity to share our faith and bring others to Christ. Then we shall describe ways of leading them into a relationship with Christ.

(a) *Intention.* One of the main reasons why so many Christians fail to lead others to the Lord is that they have no serious intention to do so. It is therefore necessary at the outset to face this question—do I seriously intend to commit myself to the attempt to win others for Christ? Without such a fixed, settled intention little is likely to happen; but given such a single, steady aim all difficulties may be overcome and every opportunity used to the full. It is of little value, however, to make a vague general resolution to win others for Christ; something much more definite and explicit is required—what Henry Trumbull, a great pioneer in this work, called a 'life resolve'. Most of us are probably unable to form deep friendships with everyone we know. One way of forming the right intention is this: ask God to give you the names of the persons you should attempt to win and then (in an attitude of prayer) form the serious intention of bringing them to Christ however long it might take. Apart from a definite rejection of Christ by the friend concerned, be prepared to persist in your intention, like the Good Shepherd who 'seeks until he finds'.

(b) *Intercession.* The Holy Spirit alone can win any person for the Lord Jesus Christ, for only he can give new life; only he can scatter the darkness of the unbeliever's night and make 'the light of the knowledge of the glory of God in the face of Jesus Christ' to shine in the mind and heart. We can do things, but we cannot do anything effectively apart from the activity of the Holy Spirit. The beginning of wisdom in personal work is the recognition of this act; the Spirit must prepare the soil or the seed is sown in vain. But this work of the Holy Spirit is done by him through us, and, as we depend upon him, so he too depends upon our co-operation. Our co-operation with the Holy Spirit is through prayer, by which his life-giving energies are made to operate more fully in the life of our friend. And so the second point in winning others is this—pray persistently for the person.

(c) *Initiative.* The command of the Lord Jesus is—'go', we must take the initiative, and 'go out' and get in touch with non-Christians. The sower 'went out' to sow his seed (Matt. 13:3); the shepherd goes after the sheep which is lost (Luke 15:4)—he did not sit in the fold and wait for it to come to him. We must take the initiative. This point is simple but funda- mental. Nothing is likely to happen otherwise. The next step therefore is this—take the initiative in opening up conversation and in 'making friends'; go where your friend is, and endeavour to establish friendly contact. In practice this may often require considerable ingenuity, and we shall need to act on the Lord's words, 'Be as shrewd as snakes and as innocent as doves' (Matt. 10:16).

Often, of course, we find ourselves aleady in touch with non-Christians in the home, at work, in social life; but sometimes it's necessary to make contact, and this cannot be done without initiative and the spirit of adventure. In this connection caution is the deadly sin. We must be ready to step over our reserve and fear of rebuffs, and take risks for Christ's sake.

(d) *Identification.* Our Lord Jesus Christ not only came to seek us, but he also became one with us, sin apart. 'He became what we are, in order that we might become what he is.' We too must identify ourselves with those we desire to win. 'Your attitude should be the same as that of Christ Jesus, who... made himself nothing, taking the very nature of a servant, being made in human likeness' (Phil. 2:5–7). Now in practice this means that by sympathy and imagination we must seek to enter into the lives of those we long to see become Christians; as it was said of Ezekiel, 'he went and sat where they sat'. Try to stand in your friend's shoes, to see life as he or she sees it, to become one in all respects (apart from sin) with that friend. This is the fundamental principle of personal evangelism; it is God's own method in the Incarnation itself. It is stated by Paul the evangelist, 'I have become all things to all men so that by all possible means I might save some' (1 Cor. 9:22).

A minister longed to win tramps for his Lord, and so he changed his clothes, putting on the rags and taking the stick of a tramp and went on the road to share that life. He walked with them, talked with them, begged for crusts, slept where they slept, and was even infested with certain little creatures! He became acquainted with the tramps' hardships and sins (which he did not share) and was able to 'save some'. We must be prepared to do the equivalent of that with anyone for whom we are concerned.

(e) *Interest.* Identification means approaching the other person

90

along the line of his or her interests, rather than the attempt to impose one's own interests upon that person. The latter is a mistake frequently made by those who attempt to win others. Approach and contact your friend along the line of his or her interests. These interests should provide us with our topics for conversation and our points of contact. If for example you know that your non-Christian friend is interested in the local football team, gardening, cooking, music, etc., then get him or her to tell you about these things, and show interest. This is the best and quickest way to the confidence of the other. It's the right answer to the question frequently asked, 'What can I talk about?' So find out about the other's main interests, encourage him or her to talk about them; and, in so far as they are innocent, go and share in them.

One final word of warning may be needed. We are not to view other people simply as potential converts, as 'scalps' to be added to our collection. We will follow the example of our Lord and Master and value people in themselves. Although we *must* befriend those whom we want to bring to the Saviour.

3—Leading someone to Christ

It is natural for us as Christians to long that all our friends will come into a personal relationship with Jesus Christ as Saviour and Lord. It should be our deepest desire that God will use us to help them come into such a relationship; we shall now describe five steps by which this may happen.

(a) *Confidence.* In using this word, we are not adding anything new, but simply summing up all that has been achieved so far. By means of that outgoing love and friendship which we attempted to describe in the previous section under 'the five I's' it is possible to win the unbeliever's confidence and trust. This is the indispensable preliminary, and no attempt should normally be made (there are exceptional circumstances) to speak about Christ until this has been done. To put it simply—make friends first, and the natural human friendship itself will be the channel through which the other is brought to Christ. The farmer prepares the soil before he sows the seed; the soil of the human heart is softened up by natural human friendship and prayer before the seed of testimony to Christ is sown in it.

Now the winning of a person's confidence is not a matter of time. It may be done in twenty minutes, or it may take five months or five years. But however long it takes, make that the first aim and avoid the impersonal, indiscriminate 'hit or miss' type of work. It is always possible to tell just when you have the confidence of the other person, by an intuition of the Holy Spirit. One of the best ways to gain that confidence (in addition to those already mentioned) is to show genuine appreciation of the good qualities of the friend, and conversely, the quickest way to lose it is to criticise or condemn his faults. Hence the rule—commend, but never condemn. When Trumbull was offered a drink of whisky by a drunk in a railway compartment, on refusing he didn't condemn the man for his indulgence, but said, 'I think you are a very generous fellow.' He won his man.

(b) *Conversation*. And now the critical time has come when an opportunity must be found or made to sow the seed in the prepared soil. 'Now the seed is the word', the word of testimony to our Lord Jesus Christ. The seed can be sown by the right use of conversation; many natural opportunities arise for directing and turning the conversation in such a way that one is able to give testimony to Christ without any embarrassment. It is necessary to stress, however, that the seed is the word of testimony, and not argument. A common reason for failure to win others is argument; avoid all argument like a plague, even religious argument. No one was ever argued into the kingdom; on the contrary, argument is fighting with words, 'banging our ideological heads together', and succeeds only in alienating the other. Hence the rule—never argue! That which comes from the head at the most (sometimes) reaches the head; that which comes from the heart alone reaches the heart. It's almost inevitable that any conversation will degenerate into argument if the Christian insists on giving 'views' rather than 'news', for 'views' are always a matter of opinion and dispute. Give news, not views. Now the news which the Christian is called upon to share with friends is the 'good news', the gospel—the story of what God has done 'once for all' in the life-saving death and glorious resurrection of his Son Jesus Christ. The Christian must lead the friend to the cross of Calvary and to the risen Lord whatever the starting-point of the conversation. The starting-point will always be provided by the friend's conversation or circumstances, his needs or particular problems. As every person is unique, it is impossible to map out a course or to describe the way along which everyone must come to Calvary— the only safe rule is to follow the leading of the Holy Spirit.

Three practical suggestions can, however, be made.

(1) Very often the transition from ordinary friendly conversation to talking about the things of Christ can be made by asking a simple question. This will, of course, depend on the person involved, and on the previous conversation; that is, it will not be a 'bolt out of the blue', but will arise quite naturally out of the immediate context. But unless the Christian takes the initiative in asking such a personal question, the conversation is not likely to lead anywhere. The asking of the question is always the crisis-point in personal contacts. Simple candour is here far better than beating about the bush, and a straight question such as, 'What do you think of Christ, Bill?' asked in the right setting may be all that is required to lead the way along the road to Calvary.

(2) Christians must know how to present the way of salvation in a simple, clear manner. They must be able to tell their friends what the Lord Jesus has done for them, giving a *simple* exposition of the Cross, and the offer of a living Lord and Saviour. They must also be able to show their friends what the Lord requires of them. This of course presupposes some knowledge of the New Testament, especially of the most relevant passages.

(3) Christians should be prepared to add to the testimony of scripture something of their own experience, especially any aspects that may appear particularly relevant to the needs of those they are trying to win. They may include, if the Spirit leads, a confession of their own failures, as well as of victories won

through Christ. Such confessions, coming from the heart, are more likely to reach the hearts of others, and to make it easier for them to share their own failures or sins.

(c) *Conviction.* This is entirely a work of the Holy Spirit, '... he will convict the world of guilt in regard to sin and righteousness and judgement' (John 16:8). It is wrong for us to make a direct attempt to produce conviction; that would be to usurp the work of the Holy Spirit, who alone can convict a person of sin and of the need of a Saviour. Now the Holy Spirit does this work as the unbeliever is pointed to the Saviour, for it is only against the background of the redeeming love of God that the true nature of sin can be seen and felt. The Christian's duty is like that of John the Baptist, who pointed to the Saviour, saying 'Look, the Lamb of God, who takes away the sin of the world!' Conviction is an indirect consequence of standing in the presence of 'Christ crucified' (1 Cor. 1:23).

It must not be forgotten, however, that the Spirit does this work through the Bible and the words of testimony of the believer. The cutting and painful 'sword of the Spirit' is the word of God. Here again the right use of the Bible is of decisive importance. It can help the non-Christian to see the true nature of his sin. New Christians tend to suppose at first that they are average, decent persons, who need forgiveness only for sins, for definite conscious acts of wrong-doing. They must be brought to an awareness of their sin. They should be helped to see that their total wrongness is simply apartness from God, rejection of God's love offered in Christ. Christians can help converts to see that the real nature of sin is pride, distance from God, self-sufficiency, rebellion; but this help is given indirectly, by concentrating directly upon the marvellous love and grace of God in Jesus Christ.

(d) *Conversion.* It should be made clear to those being won that they can become Christians only by a definite *act* of acceptance and commitment (see chapter one of this book). It isn't sufficient to decide to be a Christian; something must be *done*; or rather someone must be *received*. It may help if the following simplified definition of a Christian is quoted and explained. A Christian is a person who has met God in Christ and is trusting in him as Saviour and obeying him as Lord. The new Christian should be encouraged, in a definite act, to receive Jesus Christ, God's gift, as Saviour, and to surrender to him as Lord. The best way of doing this is for both friends to pray together quietly, when the Christian might read slowly a passage such as John 3:1–18; or quote, with periods of silence, some of the great promises of Christ (Matt. 11:28–30; John 3:16; 1 John 5:11, 12; etc.).

The Christian should then pray first, making a re-surrender to Christ and asking him to receive his friend and to grant to him the gift of salvation. Afterwards the other should be encouraged to pray, in his or her own words, accepting Christ as Saviour and surrendering to him as Lord. Then give the assurance—'You are now accepted by Christ, you are now a Christian, whether you feel any different or not. For he has promised to accept all who come to him.'

(e) *Continuance.* Our responsibility has now really begun, not ended. A mother does not bring a baby into the world and then hope for the best; if she leaves it 'to take care of itself', it dies. To bring someone to Christ and then to leave that person 'to take care of himself or herself' is criminal; it is spiritual infanticide. Therefore assume full responsibility for your 'baby' in Christ, and see that he or she gets food and nourishment, fresh air and exercise. First, this means that new Christians should be encouraged and taught to establish habits of daily prayer and Bible reading without delay. Start them on reading the Gospels and give them some simple, practical advice about daily prayers and encourage them to keep it up. They will probably need this encouragement at first. (Chapters 2 and 3 of this book may prove helpful here.) Second, they must be linked up at once with the Christian fellowship; take them along with you to your church, introduce them to your Christian friends, see that they get into their homes, and become built into the Christian community. (See chapter 7 on 'Fellowship'.) Third, encourage them at once to witness to others, to attempt to win their own friends, and to take up some piece of Christian service. (Chapter 8 on 'service' will give some ideas). Above all these things—or rather so that they may do all these things—keep in close fellowship with them yourself and pray for them.

In conclusion, we ought to deal with a possible misunderstanding which might arise from the reading of this chapter. We have been analysing and describing ten stages in winning another for Christ, in order that we might understand the process more fully. But of course in life there is no clear-cut or rigid separation between these stages; one flows imperceptibly into another. Do not go to this task with the thought, 'I must do this, and then this, and then this'; rather it is all the one united dynamic movement of love.

Christ won us by love—a love revealed in his life, poured out for our redemption in his death, triumphant in his resurrection; that love alone still seeks and saves men, but it must operate through us. Love, the love of Christ, is the key which opens the door of the human heart; love is our wisdom and insight; love is our point of contact; love is our dynamic and motive. Christ's love controls us. '. . . if we have no love, we make nothing of it.'

Questions

1. *'I believe in living the life, not in talking about it.' Discuss this statement.*

2. *What are some of the things which prevent us from attempting to win others for Christ?*

3. *'Winning others for Christ requires a special gift, and is not everybody's job.' Discuss this.*

4. *What is the place of (a) prayer, (b) the Bible, (c) church, in our efforts to bring others to Christ?*

5. *'I want to become a Christian; what must I do?' Give a clear and practical answer to this question.*